C000131328

THROUGH MANY SKIES

The Flying Days of One Polish Pilot

by

Squadron-Leader Tadeusz Szumowski

Highgate Publications (Beverley) Ltd
1993

British Library Cataloguing in Publication Data

Szumowski, Tadeusz
Through Many Skies: Flying Days of One Polish Pilot
I. Title II. Szumowska, Diana
940.54

ISBN 0-948929-77-4

Errata
The spelling of people's names and of places may sometimes be incorrect. It has not been
possible to check these.

ISBN 0 948929 77 4

Published by
Highgate Publications (Beverley) Ltd.
24 Wylies Road, Beverley, HU17 7AP
Telephone (0482) 866826

Produced by
B. A. Print
4 Newbegin, Lairgate, Beverley, HU17 8EG
Telephone (0482) 886017

Cover Picture: Tadeusz with Spitfire IX.
Picture on title page: The Squadron Badge.

Preface

This is not so much a war book as the very personal story of one Polish Pilot — my husband.

During his last long illness we came across a battered old diary which by some miracle he had maintained and smuggled with him from Poland to Romania, France, Britain, Belgium and finally back to England where he was demobilised in 1948. He had started writing it for the benefit of Zosia, his Polish fiancee, whom he had left behind in September 1939. He hoped that some day — somehow — even if he did not survive she would share not only his experiences but his innermost feelings.

Written under many hazardous conditions, the diary was scrappy and disjointed but as he translated it memories flooded back in a quite remarkable way. He was able to supplement fact with minute detail and clearly everything was as vivid in his mind as when it had actually happened.

He lived again the agony of being forced to leave his beloved country to continue the fight, the challenges of escaping from Romania, the perils of his journey to join the French Air Force, the dismay of betrayal when France capitulated, the strangeness of life in a beleaguered Britain. He thrilled again with the excitement and elation of air battles, so often against the odds. He laughed again at happy moments with his comrades and the times when authority was outwitted. He knew again the shame of some of his antics when sheer frustration drove him beyond the bounds. He wept again with longing for his own country and his own people and the final bitter realisation that the Yalta Agreement had put paid to his hopes of return.

One small shred of hope remained with him throughout the years, however, so that he never sought naturalisation but died as he had lived — an obstinate Pole.

It became plain that in order to understand his actions and reactions in times of war the training he had received as a Polish officer was vital. Part One of his story is therefore concerned with this. There was no written record but he was again able to remember everything in minute detail with all its tears and laughter, hardships and highlights which made him the man he was.

His story begins with his first steps towards becoming a pilot and ends with his last flight. His second life here in England, just as remarkable in many ways, ended peacefully on 18th September 1992 when his last battle took him in victory to the glory of the eternal skies.

CHAPTER ONE

Ground to Earth

As a small boy, I had made up my mind that one day I would join that glittering band of heroes — the pilots of the Polish Air Force. I could visualise no other future for myself and brushed aside all warnings of the difficulties and obstacles that might lie in my path.

One of the biggest obstacles was that my tastes and inclinations lay far from the academic field. Sport was my great interest and I enjoyed nothing better than the rowing club in summer and ice hockey in the winter. However, I was assured that if I did not manage to matriculate my chances of following my chosen career were nil so I set my teeth and one way and another gained the qualification necessary.

It was only the first step of the selection process and was followed by a series of rigorous medical examinations and intelligence tests but at long last I won my coveted place at the college for potential officers of all three services. This was based in a bleak, forbidding building which had once been a Russian barrack in the east of Poland on the River Bug and was miles away in every sense of the word from the bustling modern city of Warsaw in which I had been born and in which I had grown up.

However privileged and elated I and my fellow cadet officers might have felt that September day in 1934 at having reached this vital first stage of our careers, we were certainly brought down to earth with a bang. Any delusions of grandeur vanished within the first hours of our arrival. Our modish hair-styles vanished as our scalps were shaved bare. We looked like old-style convicts. It was the shape of things to come.

We were housed in bleak barrack rooms with bunk beds softened only slightly by straw palliasses and hay pillows but the life we were to lead made them the most comfortable and desired havens into which we tumbled exhaustedly at night and from which we leapt speedily but reluctantly when reveille sounded all too soon at 6.00 am. Sometimes even that brief respite was cut short for the slightest infringement of rules on the part of any one of us meant the whole group being turned out in the early hours for punishment runs and other diabolical tortures. One such infringement might be if some one had neglected to polish each of the thirty-six nails in the soles of the boots we wore to the correct standard of cleanliness and shine.

As soon as we had scrambled into singlets and shorts our days began with crosscountry runs regardless of the weather. These runs were extended daily until we were covering seven miles and more at a relentless pace with no stopping or dropping behind. To do so would invite the favourite and constant gibe of the R.S.M.

"You fancy yourselves as officers! You are clever devils who have matriculated and all the rest! What is more you actually volunteered for this! Now get on with it."

And get on with it we did. There was literally no such word as can't when applied to orders however impossible they might seem. This was exemplified early in our training when we were ordered to pick up a steel water tank approximately twenty-five by thirty feet and six feet in height and carry it to the other end of the square.

Dutifully if without much enthusiasm we did as we were told only to put it down again almost before it had left the ground. Far from relenting, the Staff Sergeant poured scorn on us and announced that we were obviously getting in each other's way so the ten tallest men among us were sent off. Again we tried and failed and five at a time others were released until we had lost twenty of our colleagues plus several more who had not done P.T. at school so were deemed weaklings. The situation was desperate for those of us left to struggle. Indeed at one time I had the nightmare thought that I might eventually be told to carry out the task single-handed.

Summoning all our reserves of strength we lifted the wretched tank and staggered with it to the designated position. We felt all in but even then we had not finished. The Staff Sergeant ordered us to pick it up again and turn it sideways to the exact position he required.

Discipline was stringent in every way. There was no free time, scarcely a free moment in days devoted to sheer physical effort as well as the mental effort of mastering all the drills and skills we had to learn.

There were no excuses. Those who failed to make the grade were ignominiously expelled. There were even three or four cases of suicide of unfortunate young men who just could not take it and could not live with the shame.

Our lives called not only for physical toughness but for the development of self preservation. There was certainly a strong sense of comradeship, each of us willing to help and support the others. In all the challenges and hardship that came our way, however, survival often depended on personal initiative.

My own methods tended to be unorthodox if effective. There was the time for instance when we left the 'comfort' of our barracks for day and night manoeuvres far from civilisation. We marched for long periods in columns of four with very few moments of rest or sleep except when we could find a derelict barn or huddle round a small campfire. The matter of sleep was settled by each four linking arms, the two on the outside keeping awake and supporting the two in the middle who could more or less 'sleep march' until they in turn took the outside positions.

The biting winter cold was another problem especially when our turn came for two-hour picket duty. I felt as though my blood had literally turned to ice and found little comfort in the thought of huddling on the frozen ground round the campfire.

Looking round in search of inspiration, I spotted a manure heap in the nearby field and without hesitation burrowed my way into it. It was blissfully warm and I felt very pleased with myself.

My colleagues were by no means so pleased with me, however, when it came to reforming ranks before marching off once more. I might not have been aware of the stench coming from my manure-impregnated uniform but they certainly were and did not hesitate to make comments which were frank rather than friendly. I was hustled right to the back.

Actually I unexpectedly found favour again. Our officer, who was mounted on horseback, was accustomed to using his nose to assess the physical state of his men and the smell of my uniform sounded the alarm for him so that he ordered an immediate return to barracks.

By the end of the year those of us left on the course had became tough and fit in mind and body. We had been built up by food which was plentiful if spartan, by physical effort which had stretched us to the limit and beyond. Above all was the knowledge that there was nothing — absolutely nothing — which we were incapable of doing or facing if and when the need arose.

Hard as it undoubtedly was, our training was to be put to the test in the years ahead when our very survival depended on the lessons we had learned.

At the end of the year we were joined by reservists on their annual exercises and felt we might once more be acknowledged as part of the human race. If we thought our ordeals were at last over, however, we were in for a rude awakening. I had another lesson to learn — the conquest of fear, particularly fear of the unknown.

Drawn up on parade, I was horrified to find that my chief duty in the weeks that followed was to be in charge of the horse pulling the wagon on which the gun, ammunition and other supplies were to be transported on the long march to Warsaw. How gladly I would have changed places with my colleagues in charge of the wagon or those appointed to other duties but I hadn't a chance. No one asked if I had any qualifications for the job and no one cared that never in my life in the City had I been in close contact with a horse.

And such a horse! He was big and he was baleful and when I presented myself in his stable he made his feelings for me all too clear by baring his hideous yellow teeth and kicking out at me. I used my initiative and fed him my bread ration which he condescended to take, but when not a crumb more remained his reactions were just as they had been.

Sick and shaking with fear, I retreated to safety. God was on my side as He had been so often and would so often be again. One of the reservists who was of peasant stock saw my plight and enquired what was the matter. He promptly offered to return with me to the dreaded stable, cursed the horse, cuffed him, kicked him where it would hurt most, and had the tack on before the animal had chance to object.

"Animals smell fear and play up." I was told. "Show him who's boss. He might be a lot bigger and stronger than you are but he's too thick to realise that."

I found it difficult to believe him but had no choice. By a mixture of bribery, bread — which he loved — and bravado, the horse and I struck up a working relationship and in the end I was quite sorry to part company with him.

Eventually we and the reservists were formed into a training battalion at full strength and the long march to Warsaw began. Day after day we marched through all types of terrain, sometimes fording rivers which cost one or two lives when those too exhausted and confused to take the right path were swept away and drowned. Discipline was such that even in their extremity they were too frightened to call for help.

Eventually we reached the outskirts of Warsaw and were

Tadeusz in his first uniform as a trainee in 1934.

4

able to fall out and spruce up in conditions which, however primitive, seemed the height of luxury after all we had been through. It was August and scorchingly hot and our uniforms were sodden with sweat for there had been no let-up in the relentless pace. Now we were once more impeccably turned out as befitted representatives of the Polish Forces. Feeling almost human again, we were formed into columns of four to march into the city centre following the cavalry, the tanks and the guns. How proud we felt as, tiredness temporarily forgotten, we marched through streets lined with people. We even sang as we marched and our blistered, aching feet stepped out with a will.

In the heart of the city, on Jerozolimska Aleja, podiums had been erected and on these stood an impressive line of Marshals and high ranking Polish officials with their eyes fixed on us.

On me! I was so bursting with pride that I could for the moment forget the agony of my right foot, the sole of which had become one gigantic blood blister. When the parade was over this was to be examined with horror and to lead to my being consigned to an ambulance.

That was later, however, this splendid moment was now. Amongst that august official assembly was a corpulent figure resplendent in a white uniform with row upon row of medals glinting in the sunshine. He was none other than Herman Goering! Germany and Poland had concluded a non-aggression pact and he was representing the great Reich. How ironic it seems that on that August day in 1935 we saluted him and paid him due homage! How little we knew that the day would soon come when our attitude towards him would be different indeed.

We had come through our first testing year. It was all over and at last — at long last — we could put it all behind us and concentrate on the joys of being reunited with family and friends. We could take up again the carefree lives we had left behind us. For a whole glorious month we were on leave.

CHAPTER TWO

A Glimpse of the Sky

Leave was even better than I had anticipated. My mother, family and friends fell over themselves to spoil me and to show the pride they felt in me. I must admit that I was quite proud of myself that I had come through the year a bit battered but unbowed and all the hardships I had endured seemed in retrospect to lose their terrors and in a strange way even to inspire a certain warmth and value. I enjoyed being the centre of attention and telling my story to attentive ears. Even my rich Uncle Lampe who had never shown much approval of me before took me to dinner in one of the best restaurants where there were several fully-fledged officers amongst the diners giving me the chance to show off my salute and be acknowledged as a member, however humble, of the same company.

It would take a bit of doing, I felt, to take up again my role as the lowest of the low, although another part of me — the major part — longed eagerly to go ahead with my training and reach the next rung of the ladder which would eventually take me to my goal.

I had been ordered with my fellow cadets to Ustjanowa, a remote district high in the foothills of the Carpathian mountains, where we were to spend about three months learning to fly gliders. On the railway line to Lwow we turned off the train at Kolomija where we changed to small trains designed for the narrow-gauge railway which led up the mountains. They were far from modern with wagons of tree trunks and primitive windowless carriages in which we stood. The engine had a special chimney belching out smoke which was topped by a large circular disk for all the world like an outsize kitchen colander in which sparks could be trapped to avoid the danger of trees being set on fire. Although the actual distance covered was not great it took an hour and a half as the train chugged its way ever upwards through the trees until finally we had arrived at our next 'home'.

We were all a little apprehensive as to what this might be like after the grim barracks we had left but soon found this to be unfounded.

6

Set in a wide clearing amongst the trees were two large huts, one to be our dormitory accommodation and the other our mess with dining-room, classrooms and so on. There was a smaller separate building to house the staff. The air was full of the scent of pine trees and the peace and silence everywhere emphasized just how far we were from the hustle and bustle of life. Some of my companions used only to city life might have found it a bit lonely and intimidating but my heart sang with the memory of so many Scout Camps where I had spent some of the happiest times of my life.

We were all happy when we saw our dormitories. There were real beds instead of tiered bunks and although we still had straw palliasses and hay pillows there were actually sheets and pillow cases not to mention small lockers beside each bed holding — believe it or not — bedside lamps and a wardrobe each.

We were even more pleasantly surprised to find that our days of queuing up with our tin plates for food had ended. We sat at tables now and were waited on by mess stewards, and the food was well-served and varied whilst still being as plentiful as before.

Another joy was that reveille was advanced an hour to the much more civilized time of 7.00 am and although we still had to shoot out of bed in a hurry and take part in pre-breakfast runs, some consideration was given to the weather and when it was really bad we were spared. Altogether we began at last to feel that we were cadet officers, however lowly, and not mere worms to be ground into the earth if ever we dared to lift our shaven heads. Although discipline was still strict we had already learned to do everything we were told at the double and without question and our instructors devoted their efforts to giving us the essential skills we needed rather than trying to rob us of what wits we might otherwise have had.

We were there to take our first basic steps in learning to fly even though this meant flying only gliders and pretty basic ones at that. Few of us had even seen a glider let alone had close contact with one but our training was carefully planned and step by step we were given confidence. In the classroom at first we learned about gliders and the principle on which they worked before examining the real thing. We learned the basic elements of meteorology, too, and other subjects highly relevant to our future careers. The gliders we had at our disposal were so flimsy that they were little more than gigantic kites with plywood frames, cloth-covered wings and a seat only just adequate for our tough muscular frames. We were, however, duly impressed and entered enthusiastically into the business of learning to fly them.

During our first few lessons our instructor was the pilot and our job was to man the elastic ropes fastened in V shape from the front of the glider. There were twelve of us on each rope and we had to run faster and faster until the speed reached was sufficient to launch the glider which

Tadeusz in 1935. In the second year of his training gliders were used before moving on to powered craft.

took to the air from the slope of the hill and landed in the clearing at the bottom.

Eventually it was our turn and I was secretly glad that my surname was in the second half of the alphabetical order so that I could watch my colleagues and hopefully learn from them. It was a fantastic moment and one which I shall never forget to find myself airborne for the very first time although I had scarcely time to relish it before landing with a jolt on the ground.

Our next stage was to learn to control the glider with left and right turns. Now we moved higher up the mountain and the clearing below was dominated by a solitary fir tree. How haunted we were by that tree which seemed to reach out its branches to entrap us. It succeeded too on many occasions when various colleagues moved a little too close with disastrous if not too serious effects on themselves and the gliders. The odd broken arm or collar bone was nothing, however, to the scorn heaped upon them and those lucky enough to escape in the ambulance to the nearest hospital felt they had come off best. More by luck than judgement I avoided such collisions.

Those of us who had mastered the elementary skills moved during the last week or so to 'proper' gliders in which we could learn the art of sailing, using air currents and aware at last of the utter, glorious feeling of leaving the world which we knew and drifting through the great silence of space. It was a joy almost impossible to describe to see the landscape gently unfolding beneath us and not only to see but to hear the voices of earthbound mortals who paused in their work in the fields to wave a salute.

Our three months at Ustjanowa passed so quickly. We had still worked hard, still been subjected to discipline, but now we were men rather than vermin and dared to believe that one day we might indeed be officers. Even here we had shed the crude dress of that first punishing year. We were cadet officers with reasonably well-fitting uniform with the coveted yellow flash on the stand-up collar, polished buttons, and a stainless steel trim on our epaulettes and the brim of our square hats. Again we caught the little steam train to take us down the mountain but now we were not herded into trucks like cattle but had each our appointed seat in the real if primitive carriages

At Kolomija on the main line to Lwow we stood, proud and expectant, waiting for the train which would take us to Deblin where our actual training as pilots would commence.

The dashing cadet officer proudly wearing his distinctive uniform with the yellow flash on the collar.

CHAPTER THREE

Climbing Skywards

After a brief leave at the end of the gliding course we found ourselves at last at the central flying school for cadet officers and felt that we were definitely on the way to our coveted career as pilots.

The main building was the country house of a large estate which had long ago been the home of a member of the Polish aristocracy. Little of its former glories remained but with refurbishment and the erection of a number of new buildings it had become very suitable for its new purpose.

It was on the Vistula. Fifty kilometres west of the river had once marked the border between the occupying German and Russian forces. Indeed the fortifications were still intact and the red brick fortress had been put to use as the quarters of several units of the army. The small town of Deblin was quite close and here were shops and bars which we would be able to patronise in off duty hours which, for the first time, we would be able to spend as we pleased.

It was a joy to find that whilst still sleeping in dormitories these were well furnished and comfortable and we slept on real mattresses with feather pillows. It was even more of a joy to find that menial domestic tasks no longer came our way with stewards to wait on us.

I was not quite so pleased, however, to find that our lives were still dominated by parades and rifle-drill and worst of all, long hours in the lecture rooms. There was so much to learn on a variety of subjects ranging from meteorology to Morse and including knowledge of either French or German. Our only contact with an aircraft was in the workshops where we were given a thorough knowledge of aircraft engines and the rest of it. Instruction was intensive and demanded a high level of effort and concentration. There was no room for slackness and although we were no longer bullied and insulted by our instructors they made their feelings abundantly clear if any of us gave less than a hundred per cent to meeting their exacting standards.

The first real high-spot came one day when without warning we were

The two-seater training aeroplane used at Deblin. Tiger Moths were the British training equivalent.

taken out to the airfield and saw two real live aircraft standing, a pilot beside each. They were Bregat XIV reconnaissance and fighter planes from the First World War which had been flown in specially for our benefit. It was exciting enough to see them at such close quarters but even more exciting when we were told that each of us in turn was to be taken up for a short flight.

What a thrill and a novelty that was! We had experienced the sensation of being air-borne on our gliding course but this was different. I sat enthralled in the rear cockpit as we took off and climbed upwards at what seemed to be an incredible speed, seeing the airfield and the river and roofs of Deblin below us before all too soon we had landed again. How I admired and envied the pilot and yearned for the day when I too would have at my command such a powerful and wonderful flying machine. Alas! It proved to be a one-off treat and it was back to lectures and tests and all the academic demands that I found so irksome and could only face because it was made abundantly clear that they were the inevitable and only gateway towards that seat in the cock-pit.

Christmas brought a brief leave with all the joys of home and family and friends and then it was back to Deblin and the salutary shock, as far as I was concerned, of being hauled in front of the Flight Lieutenant who

A recent (1993) picture
of the memorial to all the
Deblin trainees.
(D. Szumowska)

was our high white chief and told that I had failed abysmally in my Morse test, had only managed to scrape a pass in other tests, and that my standards of drill left a lot to be desired. Whether I liked it or not I had to grit my teeth and devote myself far more whole-heartedly to my studies or face the prospect of being ejected from the course.

To make matters worse, the pain in my groin was showing no sign of going away and was indeed becoming more severe. It stemmed from the show we had put on for the staff before going on leave. We had worked hard to make it a success, not only the show itself but the decor and setting. The gardeners had provided a variety of palms and other potted plants and it was a particularly large palm that was my undoing. I had been given the job of putting everything in position together with several of my colleagues. Patience never having been one of my virtues, I decided to move the palm myself as they were not ready to help at that instant. I felt a sharp pain but ignored it until I found a strange lump in my groin when I went to bed. I consulted our family doctor in Warsaw whilst on leave and he diagnosed a hernia requiring an operation and told me to report to the Medical Officer immediately on my return to Deblin.

Pain and discomfort compelled me to take his advice but if I had looked for reassurance I was disappointed. Of course I needed an operation, he said, whilst agreeing that this would put me back a year on my course. My plea that I could put it off until our long leave at the end of the course and that meanwhile he would give me a certificate excusing me cross-country runs and other tough physical activities fell on deaf ears. If I rejected an immediate operation it was my responsibility, he would not and could not help. Determination — or pig-headedness as the less friendly would call it — was another feature of my character and somehow or other I managed to let neither my hernia nor my need to study extra hard interfere with my chosen path. Fortune favours the brave, they say, although in my case for brave one should perhaps substitute foolhardy.

Certainly I was pleased in the fact that nothing went drastically wrong. I was able to cope with all that was required of me and to enjoy the more pleasurable side of life as well. We were free to go off on our own or with colleagues when off duty. There was a small restaurant under the main house where — when funds permitted, which was not often in my case — we would enjoy splendid meals particularly Wiener Schnitzel with mushrooms and poached eggs, with all the comfort and glamour of top-class restaurants elsewhere. The walls were hung with pictures that were caricatures of previous students.

There were other delights laid on for us such as skating when the ice was thick enough on the lake at the back of the house with the lights turned full on in the dining-room to lend illumination. Our staff, many of whom lived in quarters in the grounds with their families, were happy to join in these activities in off-duty hours and to relax with us whilst never forfeiting our respect.

Best of all, however, far and away the best, was that the time had arrived when on top of lectures we were at last given our first regular instruction in flying. Rumours had been rife for some days that this was imminent but nothing official had been said. One evening, however, we were told that reveille would be early the following morning and after our morning run, breakfast and parade we were told to don flying overalls and were marched in columns of four across to the airfield. Here were the hangars, the flying control and other offices and from the hangars six light aircraft were wheeled in our direction.

They were R.W. top-wing two seater training aircraft of a similar size to the Tiger Moths we were to meet many years later in England although of course the latter were bi-planes. A Sergeant Instructor accompanied each aircraft and we were split into six groups and told to gather round our allotted plane. How eagerly we listened to everything that our instructor told us — to observe but not to touch, to do exactly as we were told without question. One at a time we were taken up for a flight but this time our instructor told us, through the speaking tube, what he was doing and how he was doing it, warning us at the same time to keep our hands and feet strictly off the controls.

How skilled and patient those instructors were! Gradually under their expert guidance we learned to handle the controls, to take off, to steer, to land. To begin with my enthusiasm and impetuosity got the better of me and I seized the controls much too forcibly only to be told that the instructor did not want to die and had no intention of letting me kill him. My next efforts were far too tentative but at last I began to acquire the necessary feel for what I was doing and knew the sheer joy of having the machine respond to my will and command.

Flying was bliss, landing was less so, demanding fine judgement of coming in at just the right angle and lifting the nose at the split second needed to land smoothly on all three wheels. One wonderful day however my instructor ceded his place in the cockpit to the Flight Lieutenant who took me through my paces, made a few caustic and pertinent comments on my performance, and then got out telling me to take off again on my own. Feeling literally sick with a mixture of fear and excitement I set off and by the grace of God managed to land with both myself and the aircraft intact. I had gone solo.

From now on it was a question not merely of survival but of constant improvement of flying skills and familiarisation with the aircraft. Over and over and over again the same exercises were performed, sometimes the instructor watching eagle-eyed from the ground, sometimes flying with me. Nothing less than perfection would be accepted. There was the art of navigation to be acquired too following classroom lectures. We moved on to further essential techniques such as flying in bad weather and landing with a stalled engine (hair-raising, that was!) and the rudiments of aerobatics.

All the time our lectures on the ground went on but now I could appreciate them better as I discovered how vital theory was to the actual practice of flying. It was one thing to learn how to fold a parachute but another to be able to do it knowing that my life might depend on doing it correctly.

Altogether despite the pain from my hernia, I was happy and fulfilled and would have changed places with no one, certainly not with the three or four of my colleagues who proved incapable of learning to fly and were transferred to be navigators or observers.

As soon as I returned to Warsaw for my month's summer leave, I saw our family doctor and from him obtained a letter to take to the large Military Hospital. The Chief Surgeon, a Colonel, was horrified by the condition of my hernia and pointed out how foolish had been my delay in seeking an operation. There was no further delay and before I quite knew that was happening I found myself stretched out in bed with a large incision in my stomach and a heavy sandbag keeping everything in place which was the recognised treatment in those days. The pain was really severe and I was given morphine to help me to endure it.

Unfortunately, although the pain eased, my craving for morphine increased and I went to inordinate lengths to obtain supplies. How many young nurses fell for unscrupulous profession of undying devotion risking everything on my unworthy behalf! I did not realise in my folly the effect it was having on me but my instructor certainly did once I was back in his charge. He told me bluntly that my reactions had deteriorated to such an extent that flying with me was flying to the cemetery and gave me just one week to kick the habit or say good-bye for ever to my flying ambitions. I knew that he meant what he said and that far from being harsh he was putting his own career on the line by not reporting me immediately to the authorities.

I threw my precious hoard of tablets down the toilet and steeled myself for the torment I must go through. And torment it certainly was! Never would I wish such an ordeal on anyone and there were times when I thought I could never go through with it. My brain, my body, my whole being seemed to be in a state of disintegration and every small thing I was called upon to do seemed an impossible task. By the end of the week, however weak and shaky, I knew I had succeeded and my instructor knew it too.

It was imperative for me to reach peak form again as soon as possible for now there were increasing demands on our flying skills. We progressed onto more advanced training aircraft and added to our normal exercises cross-country flying, real aerobatics and firing practice. All the time we were subject to close supervision to make sure that standards were rigorously upheld and it says much for that training that not one pilot and not one aircraft sustained any harm.

One enormous source of pride and pleasure lay in the fact that at last we were equipped with blue air force uniform replacing the khaki. These uniforms were complete down to the last pair of pants and socks, fitted perfectly and — the crowning glory — included a full length black leather coat in which we felt like gods indeed.

We were now allowed fairly frequent passes at weekends and as there was a regular train service from Deblin to Warsaw, which was about fifty kilometres away, I was able to show myself off to my heart's content to my admiring family and friends. Air Force Officers were few and far between and even mere cadet officers like myself could be sure of adulation particularly from the female members of the population. Poor Zosia, my regular girl friend, must have suffered from a mixture of pride and alarm when we were out together. But however roving my eye might have been and however willing to take advantage of opportunities for dalliance, basically she remained girl friend number one and I think she knew it.

During the second year at Deblin flying took priority over most other things. We had to learn how to handle our aircraft as though they were a part of us with every move practised over and over again. We had moved onto more advanced aircraft now — the F.S.W. trainers with 220h.p. rather than the modest 100h.p. of the R.W. on which we had cut our flying teeth. Now we learned all sorts of new techniques including full aerobatics, formation flying, low flying and fighting. We went solo all the time now but had cameras fixed onto the wings of our aircraft synchronised with clocks and photographs produced could be studied very critically by our instructors enabling them to assess our prowess or lack of prowess in minute detail. Navigation too played an ever increasing role with cross-country flights demanding the ability to read the ground below as accurately as if it had been an ordnance survey map.

Altogether we had to give 100 per cent effort and concentration and it was a welcome break soon after Christmas to be sent to Zakopane in the Tatra Mountains to improve our skiing. Our climate, like that of Switzerland and Austria and other mid-European countries, made skiing a natural pastime and most of us had at least learned the rudiments although a city-dweller like me had had limited opportunities to become really proficient.

Again our instructors were patient and painstaking taking us stage by stage from the comparative nursery slopes to the demands of cross-country expeditions up to twenty kilometres. We lived in small hotels where we were treated like guests and were given plenty of freedom in our off-duty hours to enjoy the bars and restaurants and mix with civilian holiday makers. I have never been one to do things by halves and threw myself into these pleasures a little too eagerly particularly as far as drinking was concerned.

Returning to my hotel one evening I took from my pocket the revolver which I should not in any case have been carrying and managed to shoot myself through the foot. Luckily I managed to miss the main bones and arteries but my foot was in a sorry state and meant that the medical officer had to be called. He was blunt and to the point rather than sympathetic and said uncompromisingly: "You have damaged Government property which is a very serious offence. However I will clean you up and bandage you and providing you can keep going and do all that is required of you I won't put in a report."

It was a shock to be told that not only my equipment was owned not by me but by the Government but that it applied to every part of my body. Harming myself meant harming something on which a considerable amount of money and effort had been lavished and was an offence against my country. It was a sobering thought indeed and I knew I must grit my teeth and not try to back out of any of the activities that came my way. I managed somehow, although my colleagues were alarmed by the trail of blood I left on the snow on more than one occasion. With more good fortune than I really deserved no lasting damage was done and my Government foot healed to become as good as new.

Looking back, it is plain to see the wisdom of the powers-that-be in planning the programme we followed. The intense concentration of our flying training was broken by a complete change from activities in the air so that there was no danger of either monotony or complacency taking the fine edge off our enthusiasm.

Certainly on our return to Deblin we were ready to give our all to becoming the first-class pilots we planned to be. Another memorable feature of our training was the sudden practical application of what we had learned in theory in the lecture rooms such as the day we discovered we were actually to use the parachutes which we had laboriously learned to pack. We visited the parachute packing unit and had the technique reinforced by watching at close hand those skilled at the job. Then a three-engined Fokker bomber appeared on our airfield and we were divided into eight sets and told that our time had come. I don't know how my colleagues felt but my heart was certainly turning somersaults as we climbed into the aircraft, climbed to approximately a thousand feet, and saw through a gaping hole at our feet the countryside far below us.

There was no chance to hesitate. My moment came and I found myself adrift in space, clutching the handle with one hand and telling myself that I must count to three and then pull it to release the parachute. I pulled and prayed and for a moment nothing seemed to happen and I remembered thankfully that there was a second parachute that would open in an emergency. Then above my head a small canopy opened which became rapidly bigger and there was quite a jerk as my earthward fall was halted. It was a strange experience floating down to earth at the mercy of the slight wind which had blown up but before I could really register my emotions the ground came up and I managed to land and roll over as instructed, quickly gathering up the harness. Well at least I now knew at first hand what it felt like to part company with an aircraft and I made up my mind that if God was good to me that first jump would be my last.

It was not long after that that we were on our travels again, this time following the Wistula northwards to Torun which was an actual limit of the Polish Air Force. This was progress indeed because even though we remained in our training unit we felt part of the professional flying world.

We flew PII aircraft now which were actual fighters rather than trainers and embarked again on the process of familiarisation which would always be essential when flying a new aircraft. These were single-seater top-wing aircraft and there was no longer any question of being accompanied by an instructor although we were given thorough instruction on the ground and no deviation from perfection was permitted. We also flew bi-planes from Czechoslovakia so that our experience was constantly enlarged.

As well as cross-country flying we also learned how to fly in formation and how to fight, shooting at drogues towed by other aircraft, how to attack and how to take evasive action when our long hours of training really made sense. We were now treated as future officers and it seemed that our days of drudgery and hardship at last lay in the past.

In September came another complete break when we had the chance to try mountaineering, sailing or horse-riding. With the memory of rowing-club days I opted for sailing and never regretted my choice. Here on a big lake we learned to handle sail and enjoyed the change and the freedom. We were joined by men from other services and I became very friendly with one soon to qualify as a Medical Officer.

Through my friendship with him I had another opportunity to see theory translated into practice as he was called to an emergency at the small local hospital. A field worker had had a violent argument with one of his contemporaries who had settled the matter by stabbing him in the chest with a vicious home-made knife. The matter was urgent with no one but my friend on hand to help and according to him no one but me to assist him.

"You've done your first aid training so you'll be fine," he said. I didn't really share his confidence. We had certainly studied the appropriate manuals, practised on each other, and scrambled through our tests, but this was reality.

Fortunately for our patient the knife had missed his heart by a hair's breadth but he had a nasty jagged wound which had punctured the pleural cavity and needed a lot of repair. Pride came to my rescue, enabling me to play my very minor part without fainting or being sick but I was more than glad when it was safely over. I consoled myself by thinking that whatever gory mess came my way in the future at least I would not be totally inexperienced in dealing with it.

We returned to Deblin from the lake ready for the final part of our long training. From raw untutored recruits we had been transformed into extremely fit, highly disciplined young men able to fly to the required standard and to do anything that might be required of us in the defence of our country.

Now the emphasis was to be on the 'officer and a gentleman' side of the matter with the necessary polish applied. We were fitted with our superbly-tailored uniforms with all that went with them and felt that we really looked the part we were to play. We were instructed in social etiquette so that we would be completely at home in any situation. We spent long hours on the parade ground.

And then — at long last — on 15 October 1937 came our Passing Out

Parade when we would become fully fledged commissioned officers of the Polish Air Force.

We were each allowed to invite one guest and how proud I was to see Zosia, my beloved girl friend, take her place with all the rest. She had remained faithful to me throughout despite the times when I must have tried her love and patience to the utmost. Now she could share at first hand in the achievement and I am sure her eyes were on me and me alone as I took my place in the parade and marched up in my turn to have the coveted eagle on its chain pinned to my breast.

There was, I must admit, certain regret that my final place in the order of merit was a very lowly one. My friend and I occupied the last and last but one places and whilst those who had better distinguished themselves were sent for their first postings to the crack air force squadrons I was consigned to 312 Army Co-operation Unit.

I did not, however, allow that to cloud my enjoyment of the Graduation Ball or of the glorious leave which followed three days later.

I had, after all, won through and achieved my ambition of so many years standing. I was young and was ready to enjoy to the full all the many golden opportunities that existed in Warsaw of 1937.

This silver engraved shield was given to Tadeusz by his Godmother on becoming an officer.

The newly promoted officer in October, 1937.

CHAPTER FOUR

Grasshopper Days

It is no use pretending that I did not envy those of my colleagues who had worked harder than I had and acquitted themselves better on the course and who had in consequence been posted to one or another of the Polish Air Force Squadrons. It was without any real enthusiasm that after my end-of-course leave I reported to the Squadron Leader of the Grasshoppers Army Co-operation Unit at Warsaw Aerodrome.

There were six such units throughout the country and our task was to serve the various regiments of the Army in whatever capacity was required, very often when they were undertaking manoeuvres. Members of the unit consisted of an observer who was the senior flying member, a pilot who as far as I could see was more or less airborne chauffeur, and a back-up ground crew responsible for maintenance of the aircraft and of our own needs when we found ourselves in remote places far from base. The aircraft itself — the grasshopper — was far from the craft I had dreamed of flying all those years. It was very basic and out-dated, stemming from the late 1910's and was the type known as the R13 with 220 horse-power. A high-winged mono-plane with a fixed under carriage accommodated just the observer and myself in two round holes, and there were certainly no frills. The most attractive asset was the logo of the grasshopper on the fuselage! It was, however, all that we had at our disposal and my initial feeling bordering on contempt changed quickly to one of dismay when I was brought to realise what miracles of accuracy and adaptability I was called to bring about in its use.

My observer was quick to emphasise his seniority and his insistence that I gave all my skill and concentration to the job in hand — jobs should be more accurate for they were varied indeed and if somewhat what farcical at times had to be performed well. A call would come in from which ever army unit happened to be in need of our assistance and we were up and away. There were often two sides in these manoeuvres — say blue and orange — and we would be supporting one or other of them at different times. Naturally enough we would be far from civilisation in a terrain of forests and mountains and if I had failed to give a full hundred per cent to my navigation studies I had to more than make up for it now. An actual group of infantry or artillery had to be located wherever they might be concealed. Sometimes we were called upon to take messages from one to another using sand-filled bags with long streamers attached to the pocket in which the message was carried. These bags had to be dropped on marker on the ground near the head quarters of the unit involved.

Collecting such messages was even more hazardous. The message-bag in question would be on a piece of white canvas in between ten or twelve feet high posts marked with a flag of the appropriate colour. A three pronged grappling hook on a string was let down from the aircraft and with this the message had to be grabbed and drawn back into the aircraft where the observer would take charge of it and give instructions as to what must be done as a result.

Sometimes our grasshopper took on the guise of hornet when our job would be to bring home to the troops just what a threat aircraft would be in any future hostilities. We had to locate them and then drop 'bombs' which were actually bags filled with flour and coloured powder. Although not by any means lethal these would have given the men concerned a nasty shock and were particularly disturbing to horse-drawn artillery units as the poor horses would rear and bolt and cause general mayhem. I remember on one occasion coming across a group of men who had just gathered round their field kitchen obviously more than ready to enjoy the contents of the steaming black cauldron on the kitchen wagon. Our 'bomb' was all too accurate and landed bang in the middle of the cauldron causing the scalding stew to fly in all directions and to leave any that remained quite inedible. If our use as army co-operation was ever appreciated it was certainly not so that day.

Miles away from Warsaw with limited fuel we had more often than not to find a suitable field or other landing-place on which we could put down and then radio into base with our whereabouts and requests for essential supplies. Repairs to the grasshopper were often needed too for we were flying in rough country and small mishaps were inevitable. Taking off again represented a major problem particularly when we were on wet ground with a very limited natural runaway between rock and trees. If we were lucky there would be a barn or cottage or some form of shack nearby in which we could sleep but sometimes it was a case of huddling up under the grasshopper wings. Similarly we could be fortunate enough to find a small farm from which we could buy food but if not must rely on the iron rations we carried or wait for the back-up crew to find us.

On one occasion we were invited to dinner at a dwor or large country house quite close to where we were staying. The owner had been told of our arrival and was interested to find out who we were and just what we were doing. Perhaps he simply welcomed the break from what must have been a very quiet life miles from anywhere. My observer and I spruced ourselves up as best we could and presented ourselves at the front door where we were promptly invited into a very dark and spacious hall which might have belonged to the middle ages.

As I looked around me with interest I was suddenly aware of being helped off with my coat. The hands performing the service seemed a little heavy and I was just telling myself that out here we could not expect polished ways from a man-servant when I glanced round and saw looming over me — a huge brown bear! I felt the blood draining from my body and swallowed hard to hide my fear and discomfiture. I swear the beast was grinning and enjoying my reactions! The incident certainly coloured my recollection of the evening because for the life of me I can remember little else about it.

My days as a Boy Scout certainly paid dividends in helping me not only to adapt to conditions but to improvise and help myself. This was to become even more important in the days that lay ahead though I had no inkling of that at the time.

Grasshopper flying might not have held the glamour which I had visualised but it was certainly not boring and demanded rather more flying skill than I realised at the time besides the need to adapt and to improvise. Low flying, navigation and the pin-point accuracy of target work were becoming second nature to me and almost without realising it I was maturing as a pilot. That did not mean that I was any more reconciled to the limitations of the grasshopper and did not yearn for better opportunities.

Another skill I was developing was getting to know the right people and approaching them in the right way. I had always been a proud independent young man who felt that others should accept me as I was and had sneered inwardly at course colleagues who had been careful to win the favourable regard of those who counted. Now, not without secret shame and reservations, I deliberately set out to cultivate those who might help to further my ambitions when we met in the Mess during my times at base.

One such officer was in charge of the Training Unit for reserve officers and N.C.O.'s based on the same Warsaw aerodrome. Although in the first place I had somewhat ulterior motives in getting to know him, I developed a genuine liking and respect for him as he gradually did for me. He understood my frustrations and to my delight suggested that when free of Army Co-operation duties I might like to go across to the Training Unit and enlarge my flying skills by taking up aircraft of various types which might not at the moment be in use.

This, of course, was a golden opportunity for me to gain experience in flying many different types of aircraft, all with their own possibilities and limitations and to develop navigation skills. I was able to do quite a lot of night flying too which would prove of such benefit in the coming years. Most of all though, I tasted absolute freedom with no one telling me what to do and how to do it, able to fly free as a bird just as I had always dreamed of.

Gradually as I established my competence in the eyes of the Squadron Leader I was able to help in the training of pilots at the Unit. One such reserve officer had actually been my chemistry teacher when I was at school at St Kazimierz. The role reversal I found hilarious but I had no temptation to rub it in or make capital of it, mainly because of his impeccable attitude. He appeared to have forgotten entirely the days when I had been one of his less diligent and more obstreperous pupils and treated me with diffidence as a member of the regular Polish Air Force, anxious only to benefit from what I had to teach him. I may have been aggrieved that I was a grasshopper rather than a member of one of the elite squadrons but as far as he was concerned, bless him, I had achieved complete success.

My secretly hurt pride received another welcome boost when I was chosen with my observer to take part in the flying display at Warsaw Aerodrome. We put on our solo performance and shared the acclaim of the crowd who attended, a crowd who needless to say included all my nearest and dearest.

The fact that I was based in Warsaw and was able therefore to keep in close touch with my family and friends was another major contribution to the carefree happiness of those months.

We had always been a very close-knit family. The sudden death from peritonitis of my father had left my mother to bring up four children and how gallantly and selflessly she had performed her task. I was the baby of the family, spoilt to death by my elder brother and two sisters, and my poor mother must often have despaired of my heedlessness, my dislike of academic work, my headstrong attitude to life. What would become of me, she must have wondered, as she tried to instill some sort of discipline in me always tempered by love and understanding.

Now at last I could repay her in a small way for all her sacrifices and she was able to take pride in being the mother of a regular officer of that elite band, the Polish Air Force. Like my ex-chemistry teacher, she had no regard for my exact status. I wore the uniform embellished by the coveted wings and she was more than content.

Zosia, my long standing girl friend, was also delighted to have me within reach and her family always made me more than welcome. Too welcome perhaps, because it was obvious that they were longing for the day when she would become my wife. I was also resolved that we would be married and indeed we became officially engaged. I often sighed with her at the injustice of official regulations which forbade a regular officer to marry until he had reached the dizzy heights of Flight-Lieutenant but deep in my wicked heart I was glad of the inevitable postponement.

The truth was, I was having much too wonderful a time and was not really ready to settle down, There were too many opportunities for fun and adventure and I grabbed eagerly at them all. Life was my oyster and I relished the freedom after long and arduous days of training.

I loved Zosia but that never stopped me from taking an interest in other girls even if my intentions towards them were by no means serious. A colleague and I had the nefarious custom of putting our low-flying and navigation practice to use for which it was certainly not intended. There were many forests in the area with clearings that were popular with girls wishing to sun-bathe in privacy. Private they might have been, but not from the air when we had a true bird's-eye view. If we spotted a likely couple we would circle round and drop a message as on our grasshopper duties using a sand-filled bag with the message attached to its streamer. This message would ask if they would like to meet us at an appointed place and time and if willing if they would signal by waving some item of discarded clothing. The daring and novelty of this approach brought undeserved success on several occasions. We were not, however, eager for our blind dates to be too blind and my colleague, who had a motor-bike, would put on mufti and ride past the rendezvous to see just what was on offer and decide if it was worth pursuing the matter any further.

Like the grasshopper of La Fontaine's fable, I danced and sang my way through that halcyon time, squeezing every moment out of every day regardless of what lay ahead. And actually I was not alone. The whole country seemed to have adopted the same attitude to life, as though aware deep down, without knowing they were aware of it, that the happiness and gaiety were limited and must be made the most of before the long dark years dawned.

Warsaw was full of lights and music and magic with the shops, the restaurants, the theatres and the nightclubs full to overflowing with laughing people. After all, what had we to fear? Hitler had marched into Austria and Czechoslovakia but we in Poland had an anti-aggression pact with both Germany and the USSR and there was no reason why our cordial relationship should be broken. Hadn't Neville Chamberlain, the British Prime Minister, obtained a written declaration from Hitler that he had no more territorial claims in Europe?

As a member of the armed forces I kept myself trained and alert but that was more because it was my chosen job and one that I so enjoyed than for any more significant reason. With my colleagues we might indulge in speculation as to what it would be like should exercises become reality and like so many similar young men in other countries half-wished and half-dreaded that it might happen.

And then, in June 1939 came mobilisation. The curtain came down. The show was over.

My grasshopper days had finished for good.

CHAPTER FIVE

Face to Face with Reality

Like other officers of the armed forces, I had no vote lest political beliefs should be used to influence the men under our command. In any case I had never been interested in the political scene and was content to leave the running of the country to those qualified and interested in doing so.

I had been more than content to live one day at a time, squeezing every particle of excitement and enjoyment from each second. Feckless and self-centred I may indeed have been but, looking back, I would have changed very little. At least for that brief time I enjoyed to the full the glory of youth which was never to come again.

Mobilisation in July 1939 had the effect of a bucket of cold water on someone high on champagne. I was instantly sober and matured in the weeks that followed as though years had been involved.

I was by no means alone, of course. The mood of so many of the Polish people had been that of 'Eat, drink and be merry for tomorrow we die.' It was only now that we were all made sharply aware that tomorrow was close at hand. People began to collect and to give any materials they could just as, I am told, did the people of Britain. Metal of all kinds, including gold — even wedding rings — were contributed in a frantic effort to make up for lost time and prepare for the war which until then had seemed unthinkable.

The majority of Poles were Roman Catholics and religion had always played an important role even if the young, like myself, had tended to slacken off a little in religious devotion. Now the churches were full as people prayed for deliverance from the coming horrors.

I remember on one occasion walking past a small shrine which had been built and walled-off in a main square near the Polytechnic. It had always been respected and cared for but more often than not taken for granted. That day it was surrounded by a kneeling crowd of men, women and children praying and singing the age-old church hymns. Busy as I was and almost without being aware of what I was doing, I found myself kneeling with them and joining in the prayers and hymns. It brought strange comfort to my troubled heart.

As soon as mobilisation was declared I was sent for by Squadron Leader Frey of 114 Swallow Squadron and told that I had been posted to the squadron. It had always been a sore point with me that I had failed to be selected for one of the four squadrons which made up the Warsaw Unit based at Okencie and I should have been overjoyed that my opportunity had come at last. The situation was too grave for any rejoicing, however, and in any case I was still not to serve as a pilot.

Each squadron had a technical officer to be in charge of mustering supplies and equipment and supervising the necessary preparations for war. The 'crack' squadron — the III Lafayette — had a fully-trained and experienced technical officer but the rest had to rely on men like myself who had to learn the job whilst doing it and who were all too aware of the heavy responsibility involved. There was a feeling of very real urgency and spare time became a forgotten luxury. All my thoughts and efforts were devoted to acquiring, counting and checking materials, vehicles, spare parts, fuel and the rest of it and making everything ready for transport to Poniatow which was a country house some eleven kilometres from Warsaw and which had been earmarked as the operational airfield for our squadron, the Swallows, and for the 113 Owls.

The house stood between two forests with a large field between and this was to be home to pilots, ground-crew, gun-crews, defence units and those whose job it would be to patrol the perimeter and ensure security.

The pilots of the squadron had been sent away for advanced battle training whilst the rest of us got on with the mammoth task of seeing that they would be equipped as far as possible with all that they would require. The miscellaneous aircraft of the training Unit which had given me so many happy hours were also sent elsewhere although I took pleasure in interceding successfully for one P.Z.L.A. II fighter which seemed too good to reject. I enjoyed telling my Squadron Leader when the time came that the squadron's normal tally of twelve PII fighters had been increased to thirteen and was proud to be allowed to taxi it out to meet the others ready to be flown to Poniatow.

Although still based at Okencie my time was spent more and more at Poniatow where there was so much to do and to arrange. An ammunition dump had to be constructed in the forests and big holes dug for storing petrol in huge 40 gallon barrels although, under conditions of strict secrecy, I learned of a second fuel storage site. Four circular trenches had to be dug to house the machine guns which were French and relics of the First World War but still reasonably effective.

Accommodation for all personnel had to be made ready. The house itself would form the officers' mess together with the main kitchen and all the essential administration and control rooms. Flying crew and senior

These aeoplanes at Paniatow were, on 1st September 1939, camouflaged to avoid detection from the air.

N.C.O's would have their mess and quarters in the outbuildings and these would also be used for the two ambulances which the Medical Officer would use as his 'field hospital' besides their other more normal uses. Another mess for ground crew up to the rank of Corporal would be in the form of tents hidden at the edges of the forests and for them a mobile field kitchen had to be provided.

To revert to the fable of the grasshopper and the ant, my role had definitely switched to the latter. Like so many industrious ants, my fellow technical officer from the Owls squadron and the servicemen under our command located, acquired and transported all the different types of equipment and materials that would be needed trying desperately not to omit anything for soon it would be too late and it was on our luckless heads that recriminations would fall.

I was tired in mind and body to the point of exhaustion having worked day and night and could scarcely raise a flicker of a smile when my Squadron Leader sent me off duty for a few precious hours. My mother, bless her loving heart, and my brother and sisters did not pester me with questions as to what I was doing — in any case I could not have answered them. They fed me and let me rest surrounded by love and warmth and I began to feel almost human again. I wonder if they knew when, all too soon, I had to return to duty that the goodbyes we said were not just for a short time but for always.

Miraculously by the middle of August all arrangements had been completed. Vans and other vehicles were piled to their limits with equipment and despatched singly to Poniatow. It was vital that the Germans should not know that the rather run-down dwor or small country estate tucked between the acres of forest was a front-line airfield. From the air it had to look exactly as it had been previously, housing nothing more sinister than farm vehicles. Each van had to follow exactly the tracks set by the previous one so that the number involved would not show up under any aerial reconnaissance and as far as possible everything had to be hidden under the trees or painstakingly camouflaged.

In the last week of August everyone attached to the squadron was gathered at Poniatow and, for us at any rate, operations had begun. The pilots flew their aircraft in to be hidden at the edge of the forest where they were fuelled and checked to be in a state of absolute readiness at all times. Everyone knew what was expected of him and accepted the reality of life in cramped quarters lit, if at all, with paraffin lamps for even if the dwor had been wired for electricity it could not have been used to break the illusion that it was just another sleepy out-of-date country house. Telephone lines had of course been installed but made as unobtrusive as possible. Food stocks had been laid in and so had a certain amount of vodka and other drinks, but this was held strictly in bond and there was no chance to acquire any dutch courage however much we might have needed it.

I was still working flat out flying not in the air but on the old motor cycle which my brother Wacek had handed on to me in happier times and which proved invaluable as I kept a check on

Tadeusz on his beloved motorcycle at Poniatow in 1939.

28

the patrols manning the perimeter. There were also the defence posts which were permanently manned by men on 4-hour watches, the gun emplacements and the fuel and ammunition stores as well as dealing with complaints ranging from a stolen mess tin to matters far more serious. How many miles my gallant little steed must have covered through the dust and humps of the sun-baked field!

Only natural boundaries marked the perimeter for even if we had had the time and the money to acquire barbed wire defences they would have given away our secret location. It was imperative, however, to keep out all unauthorised visitors whether of the purely curious or of the more sinister variety. No one must enter and no one must leave. I was, on the odd occasion, able to take a van accompanied by fully-armed N.C.O's to purchase meat from a local butcher or replenish essential supplies, but that was all. Poniatow was now the only world we knew. We were on full alert.

PART TWO

WAR DIARY

1st SEPTEMBER 1939

At dawn on 1st September we were sitting around at the edge of the forest in which our aircraft were concealed — aircraft all ready to fly. As the sun rose and the morning warmed, big cumulus clouds floated above us. In the nearby stubble field a threshing machine puffed.

Suddenly in the Command Tent a telephone alarm sounded. Pilots delegated in advance to respond first ran to their aircraft. The ground crew started the engine.

Then a second order: "Take off!"

The engines roared at full throttle, throwing up clouds of dust and pine needles. Three at a time they took off. Those of us with no immediate job to do sat laughing and joking about what we saw as a Training Alarm. The dust from the aircraft's take-off was around us like a fog, cutting us off completely.

Suddenly as the sound of the aircraft died into the distance we could hear muffled explosions like the heavy breathing of giants. The Germans were bombing Warsaw. It was war. The heavy machine-guns which I had helped to station round the airfield opened fire.

The dust had settled and in the clear skies I saw as if in a fly-past formations of light grey aircraft. They were Germans. It was 8.5 a.m. The guns fell silent.

The dark silhouettes of our "Type Eleven" fighter aircraft came from behind the clouds. There were explosions nearby as the Germans jettisoned bombs before the coming fight. Our aircraft drew nearer and nearer to the enemy and we all froze suddenly. There was a strange dryness in my throat. My eyes stung from gazing into the sunlit skies. Deep in my soul I wasn't there, I was with them.

The sound of firing seemed to drop from the clouds onto the dry soil. A further short series and the dance began. Through the howling of engines came more and more bursts from quick-firing machine guns.

One German aircraft broke from the formation and dived inelegantly to the ground somewhere behind the forest. Cheers burst from us. Clouds began to cover the fighting. There! There! A second aircraft was falling. Believe me, Zosia, I couldn't breathe. I was trembling from head to foot as for the first time in my life I watched an actual air battle.

A short painful shout — and something clutched my heart, one of our aircraft was spinning in a crazy dive somewhere behind the trees.

Cloud cover increased as the battle moved out of sight but we managed to see another German plunge to the ground. A new spasm clutched my throat — yet another of ours was down. Now we could see no more, only hear the dying-away growling of engines saying it was not the end.

Zosia darling, I who had longed to fight had to stand and watch helplessly whilst others fought. It was quite unbearable. You may understand how I suffered.

From Warsaw only a few miles away came the dull thud of explosions and the sound of ack-ack gums. Now probably you and all those whom I loved were in danger and I could do nothing to defend you. Nothing. Like so many others I had no arms.

A mothballed relic of a P11 aircraft exhibited at Deblin. The picture was taken in 1993.
(D.Szumowska)

The P11 aircraft used by Tadeusz against the Germans in September 1939 in numerous 'dog fights.'

3rd SEPTEMBER 1939

Through the following dreadful days I saw others fighting and being killed.

I watched one of my colleagues, Olek Gabszewicz, flying slowly towards an enemy fighter. A second enemy fighter followed Olek very slowly, metre by metre. I knew what would happen but could do nothing to warn him. Olek had no radio and his concentration was entirely on the prey he was chasing. The German gained on him inch by inch. Waiting for the inevitable seemed a lifetime, I thought I would go mad. Finally I could hear a dry crack, like that made when a child runs a stick across iron railings. Pakpak-pak. A light flame blew from Olek's aircraft and it became a ball of fire and black smoke as it dived to the ground. I saw him bail out. His parachute opened. He was alive. Almost at the same time I saw another Polish pilot, Sub-Lieutenant Syszka, hit. He too bailed out but the Germans fired at him as he dangled helplessly on his slow descent to earth. Would he survive the fire and bullets?

My Colonel Pamula did not return . I have told you so much about him and you know how much I admired him. Gallant to the end he had at the last moment taken the place of a young pilot preparing to fly and had gone into the battle.

One good thing. My dear friend 'Szmonieka' as we nick-named him was safe. We got word he had force-landed in the woods some ten kilometres away. As an ex-grasshopper I was told to take a small aircraft and look for him. It was wonderful to see him. I landed in a potato field as near as possible and he hurried to meet me, unhurt but very hungry and thirsty. The aircraft could not take off between the potato ridges but we managed at last from a clover field.

Back at Poniatow the Medical Officer was operating as best he could on Olek on the dining-table in the Mess spread with a white sheet. Szmonieka bolted sausage and drank vodka from a corner of the same table. No one thought it strange. It was war.

Captain Olszewski was lost and so were a few N.C.O.'s. And I? I was still dealing with papers and tackling my other work as a Technical Officer. Like a grounded bird, I couldn't fly. I shall never forget this terrible inferno.

4th SEPTEMBER 1939

The Germans were rapidly approaching the River Bug and we had to move to an airfield near Babicie. Again I spent two nights and a day 'ploughing' like a weary ox. Again the same essential but irksome duties setting up our new quarters. I felt so thwarted as I bent my neck under the yoke.

We passed through Warsaw and I longed so much to get away and meet you if only for a moment. I wanted to feel you in my arms, to hold your little loving hands. I wanted to be reassured that you were safe.

But it was war. Nothing could come in the way of duty. I told myself that God was protecting you and all dear to me. That if I resigned myself to what I must do God would be good to me. And He was good to me.

When everything and everyone was established on the new airfield Squadron-Leader Frey sent for me and said I was to fly at last.

Do you understand,, my dearest one. At last I could fly and I could fight. I could fight for you, for those others I love, for my colleagues who would not return. This was the moment I had been waiting for.

5th SEPTEMBER 1939

I am led by Squadron-Leader Frey, flying on his left side. We are flying over the suburbs of Warsaw gaining what height we can.

The Germans are here, there and everywhere.

I turn my head in all directions. My neck hurts but I am defending Squadron-Leader Frey's tail. Subconsciously I am remembering fragments of our talk about war. You said: "If you are defending Warsaw, I won't be afraid."

Don't be afraid, my golden girl. I have an aircraft now and I won't let you down.

The air becomes thick with aircraft as we join up with the Third Division. Small groups of aircraft turn and twist. The blue tracers of bullets streak the air. A silly idea comes into my head. Everyone knows that bullets go straight so why do these tracers writhe like the tentacles of an octopus? The tracers are more frequent. I feel like a fly in the net of a huge spider.

Different aircraft are turning in the sky, German fighters as well as bombers.

Suddenly my Squadron-Leader dives on a light grey aircraft with black crosses on its wings. It thinks it will escape. I am following my captain. He fires a short series of shots into the German and breaks to the left. I can't understand what is happening but there is no time or reason to think when I can see the German pilot.

I make a small correction. I dive on the aircraft and the fuselage comes into my sight. I press the 'tit'. Machine guns positioned near my feet start to bark and I can see small blue bullet tracers lose themselves in the enemy.

The German dives steeply. I open the throttle. I push the control column again just to close with him. I fire a long burst. We are diving to the ground. My breath is nearly taken away. Zosia dearest, only at such a moment do you begin to know what life really is — when you are fighting for it.

I can think of nothing now but the need to shoot him down. Close by another Polish P.II goes into a crazy dive, fires into the German, and breaks away. I am ready to hit him, I am so furious. I growl: "Don't touch him! He is mine."

The enemy aircraft turns sharply to the right. It's a difficult bloody life he has. We are somewhere near the railway line to Bloniek. I can see I have hit him because he is smoking. Zosia, don't hate me but I am consumed with the wild feeling of killing. I howl from sheer happiness.

I aim again and fire and fire with no mercy. He is burning now. We are very low. He wobbles towards Kampinos Forest dragging a thick pall of smoke and bigger and bigger flames. No one bails out. Finally he crashes onto a little village between Zaborow and Leszno.

My little one, I hit my target! I fought! I am so happy because one's first fight and first victory is quite unforgettable. The little village is burning but although I am sorry it does not really register. This is war.

I climb up and up still thirsting to fight. I look for my colleagues but it is all over. Above Warsaw I see aircraft returning to base. I too must return.

Suddenly I see over Pelcowizna a strange aircraft. I am much higher than he is and even though my aircraft is much slower I open the throttle fully and dive, slowly gaining on him. I am level with him now and realise that I am being left behind. Like an idiot I fire a short burst. Suddenly — he is coming in my direction. I have a moment of madness. A bomber to attack a fighter! I will teach him how stupid such an idea is. I will fire at him as closely as possible.

Zosia, it is truly wonderful to hold someone's life in your hands. My own life matters nothing compare with the hundreds of lives he has extinguished with his bombs and those he may again destroy. We are very close. I see the details of his aircraft. My hand is on the firing button. I take aim.

Suddenly he seems to belch fire and my poor aircraft is surrounded by smoke. I just fire a very short burst and dive away. He flies into the sun.

I had to return. I couldn't fight head to head with a Messerschmidt 109 with its two twenty millimetre canons and four machine guns. The advantage was too great. One day if I am behind him I will pay him back.

6th SEPTEMBER 1939

Twice more I flew from the same airfield but had no more fortunate encounters. Several more colleagues were less fortunate and did not return from action.

We got the order to withdraw further east towards Lublin away from the advancing German forces.

Withdraw? It made sense. But what about Warsaw? Who would be left to defend my beloved city and those nearest to my heart? We were all completely grief stricken but orders were orders.

Do you remember, Zosia dearest, how I managed to snatch a brief visit to say cheerio to you? If only you knew how I felt! You were crushed by those first nightmare days of war and now I had to leave you to face what might be so much worse. I wanted to throw everything aside and stay with you so that at least we could die together. I wanted to take you away with me and I couldn't.

It is almost impossible for me to write of that terrible parting. I know though as I knew then that I had to leave you no matter what. Personal feelings had to be set aside for my duties as a Polish officer. You knew it too, my darling, and your love is a symbol of all I must fight for and the happiness we may one day achieve. At least if I am killed you will be able to look everyone in the eye because I will have died for Poland and for you.

Some senior officers did not see it as we do. They had enjoyed their rank and prestige. Now they had no stomach for the fight and were drowning their sorrows in drink with no belief in the future. Others like my dear, Colonel Pamulka were ready to give their lives and inspire us for battle.

It was a horrible night forging our way along roads jammed with refugees. Eventually I managed to join the Squadron near Lublin.

Again came torture. Wave after wave of German bombers darkened the skies over Lublin and we could do nothing. We couldn't fight because mismanagement at administrative level had deprived us of petrol.

My dearest, every exploding bomb exploded in my heart because I thought of similar bombs falling on Warsaw. What was happening to you, my sweet Zosia?

8th SEPTEMBER 1939

Our Wing-Commander managed at last to scrounge some petrol. In the morning Squadron-Leader Frey ordered three of us to take off on patrol of the Wistula from Deblin towards Gora Kalworia.

I can't get out of my mind the horrible picture of bomb-devastated ground that spread beneath our wings. Everywhere smoke billowed. Black and red ruins spoke of the tragedy of small towns and villages.

We flew over the burning forest of Polawy. We saw crater after crater telling what had happened. The sun shone brightly from a blue sky, lighting up all the horrors below.

At Deblin station caterpillars of burning engines and wagons were veiled in smoke.

We crossed the Wistula and almost immediately spotted a lone assassin. An olive-grey German bomber. He was at a lower altitude and didn't see us.

We dived. At the last moment he must have spotted us and turned sharply to the right on my side.

I had him in my sights. I walloped a good burst at him. Assailed on three sides the German opened his throttle and dived steeply. I was behind him.

Zosia, for the first time I was hunting an actual man. Till then I had seen only the silhouette of an aircraft. Now in the grey opening of the fuselage where the guns were mounted I saw the light blob of a man's face. His gun spat bullets at me. I held my fire. I approached nearer and nearer. I could feel his bullets peppering my fuselage put-put-put. Then my machine-guns began to judder, spitting shells of expended cartridges.

For a moment we were so close that our eyes seemed glued on each other. I saw his face vanish suddenly inside the fuselage and the slim barrels of his machine-guns directed themselves aimlessly into the quiet blue skies.

I fired further but could see I was being out-distanced as the pilot tried to escape. I broke away. One of my colleagues dived in and fired.

The German turned again in my direction. I drew nearer and fired again.

He dived steeply. Smoke came from his right engine. He was bound to have been hit.

We were left behind although our engines were howling on full revs. We reached tree level. Between the trees sparkled the blue ribbon of the River Pilicy.

I tried to find him and fired again hoping for a lucky shot but the devil was still flying.

It was the end. We had to return. Maybe he would reach his base, maybe not. If he crash-landed our peasants would pick the pilot's bones and those of his crew dead or not.

My darling, I was desperate. I had not been able to pay back those grey flying bandits for the dead people and black-burnt rubble they had left behind.

The three of us got together near the burning town of Grojca and began our return flight as we had little petrol left. In the region of Wraki we met another German. He was so busy looking at his handiwork on the ground and delighting in it that I was able to lock onto his tail a fraction above him. I fired into the fuselage where the observer struggled with machine guns. A few bullets and he slumped across the fuselage. The pilot saw what had happened and began to take evasive action just above the trees. He flew beautifully because no matter how I tried he eluded me.

Furious, I pulled the aircraft up again and fired. There was the dry crack of some five shells and then — nothing. I was out of ammunition.

Our luck held, however. Our leader, Sergeant Kiedrzynski, brought him down just near the main road in full view of the armoured column to which he obviously belonged as Army Co-operative pilot.

The Germans fired at us but missed and we returned to the airfield. That night we were attacked by a band of Poles whose sympathy lay with Germany. Through long hours of darkness they fired at us and we at them.

I didn't sleep at all.

9th SEPTEMBER 1939

The Germans took us by surprise and dropped one or two bombs on the airfield. They obviously expected some of our aircraft to be hidden in the forest.

Luckily they did little damage. The only 'casualty' was an airman curious to watch rather than take shelter. He jumped back in such a hurry that he fell and hit his face on a tree, knocking out a tooth.

I nearly caused another casualty. I didn't pause but hurled myself into one of the small trenches at the edge of the forest. The landing was surprisingly soft and an agonised yelp told me why — I had landed right on top of Sergeant Rajca who was already in the trench. Luckily his well-upholstered frame was bruised but undamaged. I was not his most popular officer for the time being.

11th SEPTEMBER 1939

Lublin was on fire.

Sick at heart, we could only sit by our useless aircraft and continue to pray for replacements to arrive. We had no spares and no petrol.

The Germans met no resistance as they dropped their bombs adding to the flames. They bombed and machine-gunned civilian workers in the fields and those crowding the roads in their bid to escape.

We could do nothing.

Zosia darling, if the bombers had turned on us, I doubt if we would have bothered to seek shelter. That is how low our spirits were.

Colonel Pawlikowski ordered me to take our R.W.D.S. communication aircraft to collect the officer commanding road transport and take him back. They had urgent future strategy to discuss. When I landed on my return the airfield was deserted. There were just a few damaged aircraft here and there amongst the trees. Everyone had gone.

Not quite everyone. Cadet-Officer Mierzwa hurried to me with the news that we were both to stay put. If possible a lorry would arrive with mechanics and necessary spares to try and salvage our remaining aircraft. If it didn't come we were to destroy the aircraft and fly out together in the R.W.D.S. to Mlynowa which was further east.

It was getting dark. We were cold, hungry and miserable. In the near distance we could see the fires of Lublin. We could hear the crump of artillery fire and the rattle of machine guns from the other side of the Wistula and the Bug.

We lay under the wing of an aircraft and tried to sleep but it was impossible. Where exactly were the German forces? At any moment we might find ourselves surrounded by the enemy. We were completely alone.

12th SEPTEMBER 1939

We managed to snatch a little sleep by dawn. It seemed to be growing quieter, or perhaps utter exhaustion had caught up with us. About 5.00 am Sergeant Semulewski arrived with a lorry and some mechanics.

At last !
Cadet-Officer Mierzwa went off to forage for food of some kind and I did my best to help the ground-crew in their urgent efforts to repair at least one or two aircraft.

By lunchtime the three least-damaged aircraft were ready. The others were beyond repair except for one with a torn-off horizontal tail-plane. We didn't know how much time if any we had left.

Colonel Paw-likowski returned with two extra pilots to fly off the repaired aircraft. He saw me in my torn, filthy uniform with an even filthier oil streaked face and

Ready for action on home soil.

hands and must have sensed how desperate I felt.

He didn't praise me. He didn't attempt to cheer me. He laughed. Yes Zosia, he laughed and reminded me that in the past which seemed another world ago, he had given me three days' extra duties for not being immaculately shaved. I told him my appearance now would merit three weeks' extra duties at least and actually managed to smile.

He told me if we hadn't managed to finish all we could do by evening we must all go to Mlynowa without delay, destroying any aircraft in whatever condition that remained. Mierzwa would go in the lorry whilst l flew the R.W.D.8. If we managed to salvage another aircraft I would fly that and Mierswa the R.W.D.8.

I walked around the aircraft with the torn-off tail-plane. Could it possibly be repaired? Sergeant Wojcik thought it could and we all set to work frantically. A tail-plane was salvaged from one of the aircraft that were totally beyond help. I worked as the most junior mechanic doing what I could to follow the directions of those who knew. Rank no longer existed. I was one of the lads as we ate Mierzwa's food whilst we worked. I could think only of the joy there would be if the squadron had one more aircraft. The bolts did not fit, but Wojcik found some of the same dimension and length. He said it would be all right. I was not sure but in a spirit of hope I painted our squadron badge — a black swallow on a white triangle — and 13 for the special date.

Truly, Zosia dearest, I felt I would be killed taking off in such a patched up aircraft but I had to put a brave face on things. Everyone had worked so hard. I couldn't let them down. I waved cheerio from the cockpit as I took off. I reached Mlynowa safely and landed very gently. I was afraid my little swallow might lose some precious feathers and be unable to fly.

Fine! The Colonel was delighted and said that in the morning I could return to try and cannibalise another aircraft. He was always an optimist!

All my colleagues at Mlynowa were tired, hungry and sleepy. We went to Jablorma, the estate nearby of a Baron whose name I forget. His butler brought us water to wash in, mugs of unsweetened tea and thick slices of bread and dripping.

No food in the finest Warsaw restaurant ever tasted better. One day we may pay the Baron for his meal. Feeling better we returned to sleep under the trees. We knew that the Germans were still close by.

13th SEPTEMBER 1939

There was fog in the morning when I took off in my gallant little "swallow 13" to return to Mlynowa.

I flew along the course of the road from Lublin to Piaski. The road was massed with refugees and I could see panic spreading, scattering their ranks like a stone dropped into a pond. I had the red-and-white squared Polish recognition symbol painted large beneath and on top of my wings and surely the silhouette of a PII was familiar.

Obviously they thought I must be a German aircraft whatever the signs — only German aircraft could be seen now.

A small unit of infantry was sheltering in the ditch beside the road. I flew a little lower so that they at least would recognise me.

Suddenly from the biggest group of soldiers came the flash of fire and an accurate burst from a machine-gun shook my aircraft.

God! I thought, how good it would have been if they had fired as accurately as that at the Germans.

Now I was under fire from my own side and the experience filled me with fury and frustration. I had to control myself not to pay them back in kind.

It was difficult to navigate in the fog as I flew on in what I hoped was the direction of Mlynowa . To make matters worse I had only anti-glare goggles which were of little help. I lifted them but the wind in the open cockpit made my eyes water. What could I do? If I returned to the road they might shoot at me again and this time bring me down. I grew more and more nervy but finally I managed to locate the airfield.

I managed somehow to land but the aircraft was jumping about and the tail left the ground and threw me forward. The engine was shaking like hell. I switched off the ignition and clambered out to see what had happened. I must have hit a ridge during the landing because half the blades on my airscrew were broken or missing. A few centimetres from the cockpit where I had been sitting were unmistakable bullet holes — made by Polish bullets!

It was too much for me. I sat on the wheel and cried.

One of the mechanics ran to help me and I tried desperately to repair the damage but it was useless. I had been so happy in the resurrection of my Swallow 13 which I had worked so hard helping to patch up and which I had returned so proudly to my squadron.

Now I had to perform the final act. I fired into the petrol tank and lit the spirit which spilled out.

The ground-crew had managed to piece together another PII and I climbed into it whilst Mierzow and the mechanic got into the R.W.D.8. We flew off to rejoin the squadron.

Below us on the airfield smoke rose in a column from my little Swallow. It was so painful to see. I had tried so hard but it had been rubbish before our day's work and now it was rubbish again.

I flew along the railway line to Helm where as before was all-too-vivid evidence of German attacks — burnt-out trains, holes where lines should have been. They were bombing at will now. There was no one and nothing left to stop them. I looked at my petrol indicator. Sergeant Rajca had done his best but he had no more petrol and now a bare 80 litres remained.

I reduced revolutions as far as possible and flew towards the airfield at Strzelc — perhaps they would have petrol. I reached Strzelc and met a few former colleagues from other squadrons but no one had any petrol. Desperately I drained into a bucket drops that remained in the empty barrels and poured them into my tank.

I took off again flying along the railway line because I dared not deviate by so much as a foot. I must join Squadron Leader Frey and the others so that they could have one additional aircraft.

All the roads swarmed with refugees who again panicked at the sight and sound of an aircraft even if it was only an old crock of a Polish aircraft full of holes. Luckily this time no one fired.

Only a few kilometres further — would I ever reach Strzelc? Suddenly there it was! I managed to reach the edge of the estate, touched down, and taxied towards some corn stacks. Puff-puff-puff. The airscrew stopped turning. I taxied slowly to the squadron some 5 kilometres away. I had measured everything to the last drop like a chemist. Oh Zosia, I believe in my lucky stars and in the prayers you must be making on my behalf. I reached my target. I was with my Swallows again.

Sergeant Rajca, that good man, fed me and let me sleep for I was as emptied as my petrol tank.

When I awoke I counted our aircraft. There were two from Cracow, four Owls, and four Swallows if the shaky one I had flown in was counted. That was the whole Wing. We had also three or four lorries.

In the evening a new order came. The German advance was quickening. We had to fly off again, this time to Breszano further east near the Russian frontier.

14th SEPTEMBER 1939
My dearest Zosia, I am writing this with my heart's blood hoping and praying that if I do not return you will get these pages and that you and others will understand.

We are doing nothing — we can do nothing. We can only sit here at Breszano beside our unserviceable aircraft and wait — for what? We have only enough petrol to take us one more stage on our retreat eastwards and then it is the end.

General Rydz Smigly — Chief Commander of all our forces! Our other high rank leaders whom we trusted and admired! You have led us only to destruction.

Could you not see as you sat in your splendid uniforms in your comfortable offices that we were in urgent need of petrol, of equipment, of reliable modern aircraft in order to face the might of the Germans? Did you not care as you fled to take early shelter in Romania what was happening to us? So recently we pilots were the hand-picked darlings of the Forces but you have abandoned us.

Our Warsaw Unit can do nothing to defend our beloved city which is now beleaguered and suffering God knows what. We won't give up. We are united. We want to fight till our last breath.

A bird — even the mighty eagle — cannot fly on broken wings. Our wings have been broken indeed with so many men and aircraft lost and nothing to replace them. Here at Breszano we have been joined by a few colleagues from other units who have managed — God knows how — to borrow one or two reconnaissance aircraft and to collect a little petrol from bombers and other aircraft lost in the forests. Tadek Sawicz took off with orders to Warsaw. Janek Borowski returned from a fight with large

WARSAW

DEBLIN

PRIPET
MARSHES

LUBLIN

R. WISTULA

R. BUG

R. SAN

LWOW

USSR

BUCZACZ

CZECHOSLOVAKIA

STANISLAWOW

KOLOMAZA

KUT

ROMANIA

AREA OF BATTLES   1ST-17TH SEPTEMBER

Map showing the Polish bases mentioned in the account of the 1939 September fighting against the invaders of Poland

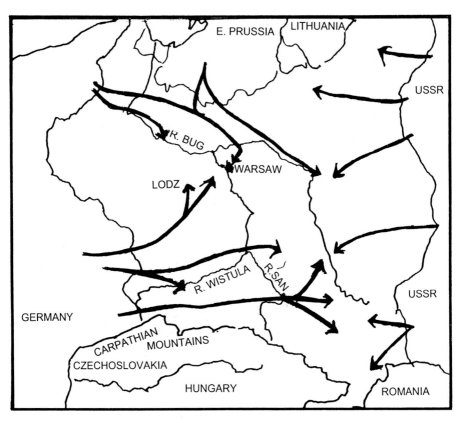

GERMAN ATTACK   1ST SEPTEMBER, 1939
RUSSIAN ATTACK   17TH SEPTEMBER, 1939

*Map showing the main lines of attack made on Poland by Germany and Russia in
September 1939.*

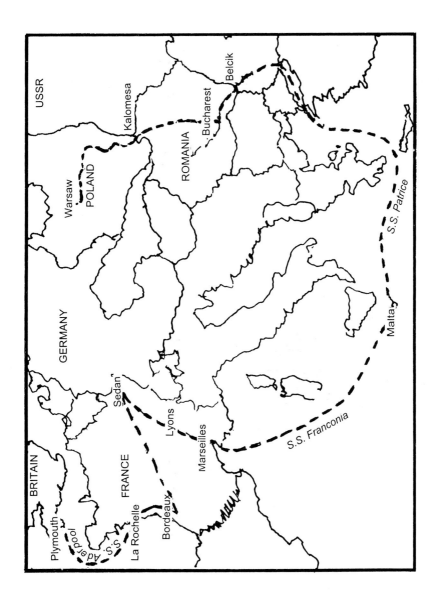

Map showing Tadeusz's sea route from Balcik to Plymouth via Malta, Marseilles and La Rochelle between 4th November 1939 and 10th July 1940

holes torn in his wing from 20 millimetre canons. Klimek Dudwal had the shield immediately behind his head cut off by enemy fire.

Others flew with wheels taken from auxiliary starting batteries because there was nothing else to be found. And so on, and so on.

I could write about air-screws which were mended with shaped pieces of wood hammered into the holes. About shock-absorbers tied up with barbed wire. About flying with torn-off horizontal tail-planes.

But I can write no more. I can only pray that God will somehow save our beloved Poland, our Warsaw, and you and all those others whom we love so much.

15th SEPTEMBER 1939

We were flying again, this time to Buczacz. We had no maps so we must fly in formation.

My worn out P7 aircraft was very reluctant to start. Finally it stuttered to life.

One by one the others took off and now it was my turn. I opened the throttle and began to roll forward but it was soon obvious that I wouldn't be able to take off. There was no power in the engine.

Just before I reached the end of the airfield I braked, turned round, and tried again. In my agitation I tried all sorts of tricks and hoped it was not just in my imagination that there was some improvement.

The others could wait for me no longer and flew off. I was determined not to be left behind again. I would be like a tethered goat with the Germans within a few kilometres already.

I taxied again to the end of the airfield and onto a potato field beyond. I bounced over some big ridges. Surprise surprise! I was airborne! That was all that could be said for the engine was labouring at barely 13,000 revs.

I could just see my fellow pilots as dark specks against the cumulus clouds. I knew I couldn't catch them as my 'fighter' refused to exceed 120 kilometres an hour.

I marked myself a course using the aircraft compass and strained my eyes in an effort to keep the others in sight. It was useless. I had lost them completely. Hard luck! I could only keep on course and look for a landing-ground.

It was such a lovely evening and incredibly I seemed to have flown into another world altogether, one where all the ugliness and horror of war no longer existed. Below me were forests, ravines and a small river. Little towns and villages lay quiet and peaceful as always with no burning buildings, no craters.

There was a wide river in a deep ravine with a railway bridge over it.

Had I flown too far? I could see a piece of level ground near a road. I landed. I would have to use my tongue as a Polish compass, as the saying goes, and make enquiries.

I had to summon up some Russian-ised Polish words in order to talk to the peasants who came up to me. I was near Horodenka, they told me — Buczacz was back in the direction from which I had come.

My spluttering aircraft again took off. I saw a little town and had the same old problem — finding a place to land. Buczacz was quite near, these people told me. It was just over a small hill. Again I managed to get airborne and in a few moments I saw Buczacz. I landed yet again and asked for Petlikowce which was the actual airfield. An old Russian gave me directions as though I had been driving a van — across the ravine, part of a forest and a river.

Somehow, my Zosia, you and your love must have worked miracles. At the end of the forest I saw — aircraft! I brought my faulty aircraft to land with a fervent prayer of thanksgiving. Squadron-Leader Frey would not be amused, I thought, and my colleagues would laugh at me, but I was past caring.

My reception was just as I had thought. No one thought much of my skills in flying or in navigation and even less of my aircraft. At least I had joined up with them again and a faulty P7 was better than no aircraft at all to swell our meagre total. We were to go to a house on the estate for the night, I was told, and we set out without delay to find it.

I saw clean sheets on a bed and a table beautifully laid-out for dinner.

For the first time I was aware of the filthy, dishevelled state of myself and my uniform after all we had been through and pride insisted I do something about it. I ran to the river and scraped off a few layers of dust and dirt but was hardly the smart young officer I had been so short a time ago.

Can you imagine how I felt? We were given a well-cooked well-served meal and drinks which were strong and tasted of honey — fantastic! After the meal the host actually suggested we should play bridge!

How I kept awake I don't know but managed to play in a semi-conscious state. Then thankfully I could go to bed where I dropped asleep almost before my head touched the pillow. Was the war and the devastation and the heartbreak we had been through just a nightmare?

16th SEPTEMBER 1939

We were busy all morning reorganising the Unit.

One part, it was decided, would go to Romania for the new aircraft awaiting us and the rest would return to fight in the region of Lublin in the least dilapidated of the aircraft that we still had.

Gradually the rest of our road transport joined us and the ground-crew worked flat out to make those precious few aircraft we had as serviceable as possible. If there was any fear or trepidation in the hearts of the pilots who were to fly them they kept it well hidden. We all clung to the hope of being able to fight again and to avenge all that the Germans had done and were doing to our country.

I was not one of the pilots selected but more or less reverted to my previous role of Technical Officer. Colonel Pawlikowski told me I was to go to Stanislawow for petrol, and I set about selecting my team of drivers, mechanics and so on who would be able to effect running repairs and keep our vehicles moving.

We were again amazed at how normal and peaceful everything seemed. The surface of the secondary roads was not very good but at least they did not swarm with panic-stricken refugees and the Military Police were in evidence rounding up personnel who had become parted from their units, keeping roads clear for essential traffic, and checking documents. It was an orderly if not a speedy journey and we were eventually directed to Regional Headquarters.

At last I saw the refinery with its huge tanks which I dared hope might be full of petrol that was our very life-blood. At Headquarters I had to produce a document entitling me to supplies and after checking received another document authorising me to collect 5,000 kilograms of petrol. Better and better! There was evidence of everything being under control.

My satisfaction at this calm control was more than a little dented when we reached the refinery. Back at the airfield everyone was waiting desperately for petrol and relying on me to deliver it as fast as possible. Here there was no sense of urgency at all. Each barrel must be weighed empty and then full before they could be loaded onto the lorries. Even after that final calculations indicated that we had received 350 kilograms too much.

Somehow I held onto my self-control and sent one of my sergeants back to Headquarters for an additional document entitling me to a full load. I told the lorries to move a few kilometres away and wait whilst I remained as a hostage or guarantor of good behaviour.

I began to feel uneasy.

Sirens sounded.

I stood between huge tanks containing thousands of gallons of fuel. I looked at the map of the surrounding area. It was not reassuring. Just beyond the chain-link fencing were military stores, a railway station, and sidings. Not far away a railway bridge spanned the river.

What a target!

There were shallow trenches for shelter but I preferred to stay where I was. I crossed myself and thought about you, my Zosia.

In the sky above I saw thirty aircraft flying in formation of three and my heart hammered in my throat. They were single-engined dive bombers and they clearly meant business.

They dived. You, my poor darling, must be quite familiar after all you have been through with the devilish howl of a dive bomber ending with the crump of bombs. Now I heard them for myself.

I was surprised that the explosions seemed further away than might have been expected and were fewer than the number of bombers concerned. People could be seen running for shelter along the chain link fencing. They called out that they were bombing the bridge but only five or six bombs had actually exploded. (Later I was to learn the answer to the puzzle — the bombs were of Czech origin and had been sabotaged and filled with sand).

What an escape!

The raid over, my Sergeant arrived with the necessary papers and we were allowed to leave. I found my lads waiting beside their lorries, their rifles loaded with incendiaries. Far from having been frightened, they were angry and disappointed that the Stukas had not come within range so that they could have had a shot at them.

We returned to Buczacz as fast as we could.

The petrol we were carrying was for road transport and not the 100 octane fuel required for aircraft but we did not let that damp our joy too much. At least it was petrol and our pilots would be able to make use of it.

17th SEPTEMBER 1939

It started out as a good day.

We had some petrol now and a few of our aircraft were able to go out on reconnaissance. The rest of us were busy on general duties. New instructions had been issued about our reorganisation. It was good to hear that Olek Gabszewicz and some of our other pilots were to be decorated for their part in fighting in the early days of the war.

There was good news too of the defence of Warsaw and the victories of General Sosnkowski near Lwow.

New aircraft awaited us and soon we would be able to fly into battle again instead of watching helplessly from the ground. Altogether for the first time in many days we were almost happy and had the occasional joke and laugh together as we worked.

About mid-day the bottom dropped out of our world.

It started when we noticed a unit of unrecognisable aircraft overhead and saw that they were dropping bombs on the forest near Buczacz. We were more puzzled than alarmed at first. Were the Germans using Czech aircraft now? We listened for news. A few minutes later it came with all the force of a thunder-bolt. The Bolsheviks were crossing the border!

Alert!

We had retreated east in order to have space to regroup and re-equip ourselves to tackle the Germans advancing from the West. Now the Bolsheviks had stabbed us in the back.

Our last orders came from Squadron-Leader Frey.

We were to evacuate with all speed possible.

Lieutenant Sawicz was to lead our remaining aircraft to land in Czerniowicze.

The rest of us must take to the road in the vehicles we had and must get together in Sniatin.

In a daze of shock and despair we carried out our orders. We were past thinking. Past even trying to understand.

By 2 p.m. we were on the road. I took my place on the eight-wheeler Krup transport found abandoned by the Germans with a broken clutch and patiently restored by our ground-crew for our use. Dearest Zosia, night is coming on us and on Poland.

The roads were jammed solid with traffic of all kinds. Private cars, military vehicles, limousines and broken-down vans were all packed with frantic, greyfaced people trying to escape. There was no attempt at order. There was no organisation. Everyone tried to find space and no one succeeded.

Inch by inch we crawled, frozen in despair, with no strength even to think of the miseries of the present or to contemplate the even greater miseries which might lie ahead.

Towards evening the skies darkened and a thunderstorm broke. The crash of the thunder and the eerie blue-green lightning flashes turned the whole scene into Dante's Inferno.

I was utterly exhausted and hungry like everyone else for there had been no time or opportunity to eat all day. I tried to pull myself together, to carry out the duties which had been assigned to me.

We reached Kolomye and I left my vehicle to try to locate at least some of the lorries of our unit. We had been told to collect at Sniatin but no one had anticipated such chaos and delay. The road ahead might already be in the hands of the Bolsheviks. Eventually, about 3 a.m., almost all our vehicles were together and directed on the road to Kut.

It was dawn.

18th SEPTEMBER 1939

Now we were taking the last part of this road to retreat. It was a slow, slow approach to the frontier which we hoped yet at the same time dreaded to reach.

The skies were grey with a light drizzle.

When we reached Kut, local people handed fruit to us which we took thankfully as it was the only food we had had for twenty-eight hours.

Three or four times on the grim journey I was sought out by a family evacuating from Malaszewcze, the wife and children of Jasia Czyz, one of my colleagues from Training School who had joined a bomber squadron. She kept asking me frantically where he was, if I had seen him. What could I tell her? I knew that very few of the crews of Losi were still alive but maybe Jasia was a survivor. I told her he was somewhere in front and eventually she was persuaded to go through.

Oh Zosia, my dearest one, one day if the good Lord allows me to talk to you again, look into my eyes and you will know what was happening in my soul. What would happen next? What would happen to you? To all those I loved?

We reached the bridge indicating the border. On a small grass area our vehicles gathered together and I met up with Lieutenant Baranski. He handed out food but it was impossible for me at any rate to eat. The pain and nervous shock I was suffering made it impossible for me to swallow.

As we were halted there, forty brand-new modern tanks passed by. They were completely unscratched for they had never been able to join the fighting. They had received ammunition for only one day.

Their crews — young NCO's and cadets — were regular soldiers. They were all crying. They screamed bitterly that they had been sold. The top people had forsaken them and gone ahead to preserve their own safety.

It was time for our departure.

Wianek Baranski still tried to delay.

Night was coming.

We all felt unreal.

My hand grasped the pistol in my pocket but I could not even allow myself to think of suicide. I felt a traitor, a deserter, but it was not my fault. It is my duty to see things through to the end.

Like many other generations of Poles, we must go West with a begging bowl thinking only that one day we will return. We drove inch by inch across the frontier bridge. We passed a Romanian soldier. We stopped. The airmen in my charge crossed themselves or cursed according to their personality. There were sudden bursts of bitter humour. Eventually there was silence.

I longed so much to sit on the bridge and howl for you, my dearest one. I wanted to cling to our Polish soil.

The fog was thickening.

I glanced across at Mazurek, our driver. He came from Upper Silesia and was always such a happy rogue. Now his face was set like a mask and tears flowed down his dirty unshaven cheeks. My eyes burned unbearably and suddenly I could feel the taste of tears on my lips.

Were they my tears — or were they yours, Zosia darling? I tasted your tears before that day at Zelaznej when like the feckless fool I was I told you that all was over between us. I tasted your tears again when we came together again but this time they were tears of happiness. When oh when will I come back to you again?

Mazurek dashed away his tears with the back of a grubby hand and pulled from his pocket a small piece of dry bread and the remains of a packet of preserved meat. He put his hand on my should and said:

"It's hard luck, Lieutenant, but it's not our fault or our wish. You must eat. We are giving way only because we have had no food. We are not women. We must be strong."

You were right, Mazurek. We were not women and we were not cowards. Somehow we would go through.

And you, Zosia mine, must go through too. The Five-Year Plan we made for each other must succeed.

I managed to eat a little although it was so difficult to swallow.

I crossed myself together with the airmen and said a silent prayer.

We passed the border sign and were on Romanian soil. It was 4.45pm.

We had been ordered to give up our arms but we hid them as best we could. I had seen the heap of first-class weapons which our infantry had been forced to give up.

We reached the little town of Wyznice and were ordered to go on, but soon after passing through the market place our gallant Krup broke down and would go no further. The other vehicles went ahead, we would catch up when we had managed to make repairs. The trauma of leaving Polish soil was behind us now and we were becoming aware of the needs of the present. One immediate need was food for we realised for the first time that we were hungry.

I went off to try to buy food but the Romanians wouldn't accept our Polish zloty which was all we had. Before the war one zloty had equalled forty-seven leia but now they wouldn't take even one zloty for one leia.

Mazurek, ever-resourceful, came to our rescue. He collected our cigarettes and returned with bread, sausage and vodka. We all drank together and felt better.

We were in the mountains and it was very cold. We had nowhere to sleep except in our vehicle so we squashed onto the seats as best we could.

Before we knew it sheer exhaustion had caught up with us and we fell asleep.

19th SEPTEMBER AND THE WEEKS AHEAD

We all woke up soaked and frozen. We made further efforts to repair the Krup but it was useless. I stopped a big Chevrolet lorry which was behind us and they took the Krup on tow. It was by no means easy to negotiate the narrow roads which snaked steeply up the mountains but somehow or other we managed to join our column and spent two days and nights in a field working hard to put our vehicles into something approaching going order.

That field resembled nothing more nor less than a car-breakers yard. Everything from cars to military transport of various kinds had suffered on that relentless journey and there were many vehicles abandoned by those who had gone ahead of us which often yielded useful spare parts. They yielded other surprises too. I was as amazed as I was delighted to find again the luggage which we had left behind in Blonia so long ago. Patient and ingenious our mechanics might be, but nothing short of a miracle would enable our Krup to take to the roads again and it had to be abandoned. We must all make what travel arrangements we could.

I came across a Fiat 508 which Wieniek, one of our senior officers, had left behind. Somehow or other I managed to patch it together and apart from needing a push start as the battery refused to charge, it served me quite well. We moved on as directed towards Storjenca where we were told we would have to leave all our equipment.

We were not as downcast as might have been expected. Rumour had reached us that we were to be interned but by no means all the Romanians were sympathetic to the Germans and there was a good chance that secretly they would let us escape and make our way to Syria. From there we would be able to go to France where there would be fresh aircraft to enable us to continue to fight.

At Storjenca we were met by what resembled a green hedge of Romanian soldiers with fixed bayonets who made known their intention to remove any arms and weapons which we had been able to get through to that point.

I had to deal with a small group of officers who asked a number of questions and decided to take refuge in ignorance and a bold front. I told them in French that I did not understand what they were saying, gave them a cheerful goodbye wave, and moved on after the column. They might have been temporarily taken aback or perhaps were indeed secret sympathisers but they took none of the hostile action which I had half-expected. As it happened all the rest of us who had acted with bravado instead of meekly succumbing to pressure had fared just as well. When we halted our column a few miles away and checked we found that no one had handed over any arms and that on the contrary our stock had increased. Somehow or other our more enterprising airmen had managed to buy or steal extra pistols and rifles whilst actually en route. By the time that evening that we had loaded any spare parts and equipment left behind by a previous column, all those travelling with us had what amounted to plenty under prevailing conditions.

We travelled for a week towards Bucharest doing our best not to be defeated by our worries and uncertainties as to the future not to mention by the hardships and rigours of our journey. Some handled it better than others and I am ashamed to say that I was not one of them. It had all proved too much and I only wanted to forget everything and find oblivion in the only way I knew — drink. It was the final straw when the Fiat which had been my only refuge, my bedroom, my means of transport, broke down and I had to be taken in tow.

Bucharest was a seething mass of bewildered Poles from civilians to the military forces and in the confusion I was directed to an Anti-Aircraft Unit who soon realised that I was in the wrong place and sent me to join my colleagues gathered at the aerodrome.

Fate had it that in the general confusion I was once more accosted by Ila Czyza torturing me again with questions about the whereabouts of her husband. There must have been hundreds like her, equally distraught, but there was literally nothing I could do for her or for any of them and the knowledge added to my inner pain and made it difficult to be sympathetic.

At the military aerodrome where we were concentrated we were able to feel like human beings again with the chance to eat and sleep and clean ourselves up. On the second day however we were ordered to leave all our vehicles and go by train to an internment camp in Goworze. The possibility of reaching France was diminishing.

We travelled in reasonable comfort but during the night the railway wagons full of our airmen were uncoupled which filled us with foreboding. We had been through so much together as a Unit and who now knew what could happen to them and if we would ever be together again. As was becoming my unfortunate custom, I tried to drown my sorrows in drink.

In the morning we were put on buses to Goworze. I was in trouble as soon as we stepped out of the buses on arrival — who should confront me but Ila! She seemed to haunt me and my sympathy was rapidly being swallowed up in irritation which I did my best to conceal. I don't know what I told her but I got away as quickly as I could and with the remnants of our squadron went to our quarters.

Goworze is in the mountains in a setting very similar to Iwonicz and Rymonow in our mountains although none of us was in the mood to appreciate the scenery. We were given comfortable quarters in a hotel and colleagues already installed there made it clear that we would be held there in internment until the end of the war.

We were held in the terrible claws of inertia, hardly able to think or feel any more. We were well treated as far as our physical needs were concerned. We had the opportunity to catch up on eating and sleeping and were not closely guarded. We could walk around the area and spend the Romanian money they gave us in the little town. We listened to the radio where we heard continuously of the complete destruction of Warsaw, the beleaguered city, but it all seemed remote from life as we knew it.

Zosia, my darling, how can I explain? We lived in limbo with all the fight, all the spirit gone out of us. We were out of touch with you, with our families, with Poland. We sent letters through the Red Cross but I doubt if they would reach you.

I took refuge in drink which only seemed to increase my misery. Indeed, there were times when I contemplated suicide and might even have attempted it had it not been for the support of the other four members who were all that survived of our squadron — Baranski, Borowski, Szmonka and Mierszwa who had been a cadet officer but who had had to grow up very fast. Days grew into weeks almost without our noticing it and despair gave way to an acceptance of our fate which was even more demoralising and dangerous.

Then, suddenly, almost without reason, the situation changed or rather our attitude towards it. We made up our minds that come what may we had to get out and become part of the fight again.

Now we had an aim, a purpose in life, and it made all the difference. We had to acquire civilian clothes and forge some type of new documents for ourselves. Inertia vanished and every minute was put to good use.

We had to provide ourselves with new identities and become familiar with all the details of these supposed lives so that we would be ready to answer any questions. Baranski became a civil servant, Borowski an electrical engineer, Szmonka a primary school teacher, Mierszwa a tailor and I was a chauffeur. At least we were ready and eager to put our scheme into operation.

We destroyed our military documents and gave a lot of our clothes to a fellow internee, the wife of a solicitor from Siedlec, whom we had got to know. She was a qualified nurse and had been called up leaving her two small children with their grandparents. The hospital where she was based was bombed, trains were bombed, and she had eventually escaped on a farm rulley. She arrived at Goworze with no luggage, no money, no coat to cover the dress she was wearing, and just one change of underwear. She was delighted with our uniforms — from them she would be able to make a suit and a fur lined leather coat, amongst other things, and the money we also gave her would buy some underwear. I also left her a blanket and gave her your address, Zosia. Please forgive me, darling, but I told her you were my wife. I wonder if she ever got in touch with you?

We left the camp with no regrets and under cover of darkness made our way to the station where we managed to jump onto a goods train. However, it was not to be as easy as all that. We were found at the next stop, taken off the train, and locked in a small building prior to being returned to Goworze the next day.

It was very dark in the building but we saw that the bottom of the walls was very wet and the smell told us that it had been used to house pigs. We dug and scratched with our bare hands and eventually made a hole large enough to let us get out. Leaving the station we had no knowledge of where we were or in which direction lay Bucharest where we knew we must be to seek help from the Polish Embassy.

We had to avoid roads and take to the fields as much as possible to avoid being seen. By now it was clear that the Romanians were very divided in their sympathies — half were pro-German and half pro-French. It was the latter who were sympathetic towards the Poles and the former who had caught us on the train and locked us up.

Finally we reached another small station, boarded another train, and this time got to Bucharest and somehow made our way to the Polish Embassy. Our reception was guarded as was understandable and we had to undergo considerable questioning before at the end of a week we were given money and tickets to Balcik.

Although we now had tickets the first train we caught had a pro-German crew and we were curtly turned off to wait for the next train whose crew was luckily pro-French.

When we arrived at Balcik, a little port on the Black Sea, we found that it was full of Polish people who were by no means welcome visitors which was understandable. An extra one and a half thousand people was an obvious drain on local resources and as I have said, many Romanians were not sympathetic to the Poles. We decided that we should no longer stay together as a group as if our escape from Goworze had been reported we would be arrested and sent this time to prison from which escape would be impossible. We would have more chance if we went our individual ways hoping and praying that we might meet up again in France. The most vital need was to find a ship which would take us somewhere — anywhere — that would serve as a base for the next stage of our journey but this was easier said than done.

Long queues formed all day and every day at the office which issued vouchers and it was a case of infinite patience and persistence. With God's help I was lucky in the end, partly because of the scar on my neck which as you know, Zosia, was the souvenir of an operation on a tooth when I was a child which had gone wrong leading to a quite severe infection. I told the authorities that it was a scar following T.B. of the jaw and the fact that I had suffered from such a dreadful disease aroused their sympathy. I had my visa! The steamer arrived. There was one more check. I was allowed to board.

Balcik, you are not a bad little place really. You are warm and sunny and must be quite beautiful in normal times. One day, when and if the war is over, I will return.

You and I, my Zosia, will return together and at leisure retrace the vagabond road which took me from you.

4th NOVEMBER 1939

The boat on which I found myself turned out to be British — the *S.S. Patrice*. It had been built as a small pleasure cruiser carrying passengers on cruises of the Adriatic and Ionian seas and islands. Around 1,000 tons, it had coped admirably with up to two hundred passengers and perhaps twice that number of crew. Now there were 15,000 people aboard and the crush was quite indescribable.

At the moment of our departure, Colonel Wieden, the Senior Officer aboard, gathered as many of us as possible around him and led us in the singing of the Polish National Anthem.

"Poland is not lost for ever . . .
    March, march Dombrowski from Italy to Poland."

The wind carried the words across the surface of the Black Sea as the coast disappeared.

Zosia darling, will history always be repeated? Must each new generation be forced into exile by hyenas hungry for money and power? Must Poland always be rebuilt on a foundation of bodies of its best people?

As the boat sailed into the open sea it began to wobble like a drunkard, unable to cope with its overladen state and the rising power of the waves. Many people were ill. I was lucky enough to find a place on the floor under the dining room table. There were airmen around who were thoroughly demoralised by the present conditions and by all that had happened. In their misery they cursed their officers, their senior officers and everyone else whom they thought to have contributed to their misfortunes. They were deaf to any reassurances or suggestions, in fact when they gleaned that I was an officer even of very junior rank they spoke of throwing me overboard both as a scapegoat and to create more room for them.

The situation might have been ugly had it not been for a small group of N.C.O's and airmen from my old platoon and the N.C.O's school in Warsaw. I felt so proud of them because they understood that in spite of everything we were still an organised unit and behaved accordingly. They were Polish airmen and I was a Polish officer and they let nothing interfere with that. The other airmen would have had them to reckon with had they laid a finger on me and they decided not to take the chance.

In the morning I and some other officers were on duty guarding the ship's galley where there was nearly a riot as hungry men tried to fight for the food which they thought might be there. In the afternoon we sailed into the quiet waters of the Bosphorus and immediate orders came that we must all go below and keep completely out of sight as the Turks were thought to have German sympathies and had they caught sight of us an ugly situation might have arisen. Through the portholes we caught the odd glimpse of the panorama of Istanbul.

It was a beautiful view but you were not there to share it with me, my Zosia. Where are you? Are you still alive? Around four in the afternoon we were handed a meagre portion of food which was by no means enough to stave our rapidly increasing hunger.

We sailed on through the Sea of Marmara and the Dardanelles and reached the Aegean. It was beginning to feel much warmer but the sea grew rougher and rougher. It tossed our overladen boat like a child's toy. Such lifeboats as there were could have held at the most a seventh of our complement and there were no lifebelts. I was starving and terrified like everyone else but managed to hold onto my self control helped I am sure by a few carrots which had been torn from the store and were on the deck. I chewed frantically on them as the waves grew high enough to wash right over the top deck. I didn't want to die slowly in a fight with the ocean rather than quickly in battle.

Night fell again and there was no release from our misery. We were literally starving despite another tiny portion of food. There were no lights on the boat and the darkness in our hearts and minds was even more intense. We had no idea where we were going or if our ordeal would ever end. Few of us could speak any English so it was impossible to get information from the crew.

Around dawn we began to trace big circles in the water and saw land ahead of us. News filtered through that it was Malta. We sailed into port but immediately a signal from the land sent us out again. Around mid-day we sailed into a creek used as a landing-place for seaplanes and at last dropped anchor.

Zosia dearest, for the first time I recognised wherein lay the strength of Great Britain — their powers of organisation whatever the conditions or circumstances.

A representative from the Royal Navy came aboard, inspected the boat, and decided on the required action. Food was obviously our primary need and small tugs came alongside bringing food of a type and quantity which we had long since forgotten — bread, tins of corned beef and other meat, butter, tinned fruit, condensed milk and jam amongst other things. We could have as much as we needed and I am afraid I was greedy — not only did I eat my fill but I hid a tin of corned beef and a loaf of bread under my ragged clothes just in case I should be hungry again!

We were told that the boat was so grossly overladen that it was folly to continue. Consequently only a few would stay on board to continue the journey to Marseilles whilst the rest of should remain in Malta.

11th NOVEMBER 1939

Moored in Valetta harbour was another British cruise ship, but what a difference from the *Patrice*! This was *S.S. Franconia* which had sailed between Southampton and New York and was about 22,000 tons. We found out that its bows had been damaged during manoeuvres and that it would be under repair for another week. Meanwhile it would be used as our new temporary home.

We were taken aboard, had a quick medical check, and then came the long-drawn-out business of identification and dividing us into our respective ranks of officers, N.C.O's and airmen. It took well over two hours as we were all filthy, in rags, and minus any documents.

As we waited darkness fell and we saw Malta's wonderful anti-aircraft defence. There was an orgy of lights as more than twenty-eight reflectors crossed and criss-crossed the skies.

Eventually as officers we were taken to the First Class dining-room for dinner. Can you imagine, my Zosia, how we felt? For so long we had been refugees, hungry and miserable, all our self-esteem gone, robbed of our status as fighting pilots, robbed of our country, and most of all robbed of all those we loved. Now suddenly we walked into a fairy world of crystal chandeliers, snow-white table cloths, gleaming table silver and were greeted by immaculately-dressed stewards whose eyes never betrayed by so much as a flicker what they must have thought of us.

The most wonderful moment of all came when the Captain of the Franconia appeared in the full glory of his uniform to welcome us. In a brief but memorable speech delivered in perfect French he greeted us as Polish officers who would make a valuable contribution to the war effort. He made it clear that he saw beneath our rags and filth and respected us as the proud pilots we had been and would be again. I learned later that he had paid similar visits to our N.C.O's and to our airmen.

It made all the difference. No longer shaky and frightened I managed to pull myself together and enjoy a truly excellent dinner of fresh salmon, turkey, fruit salad and ice cream with as much real coffee as we could drink.

We were then allocated our cabins which were very comfortable but all on the inside of the boat without portholes. This was perhaps an indication that for all the courtesy and consideration shown to us the British were just a little wary of us and who could blame them?

Our senior officers decided who was to go into which cabin and there was the endless talking, indecision, orders given and countermanded, which we had by now come to expect. Then at long last we were installed. It was a joy to find soap, razors, toothbrushes and plenty of hot water so that we could begin the task of looking human again. We even managed to wash the tattered remnants of our clothing, stretching our trousers carefully on the slats below our mattresses so that they would bear some semblance of a crease.

When we were assembled the next morning representatives from each of the six units of the Polish Air Force were there and it became possible to establish at last who was who. Each one of us was known and could be recognised by senior officers as well as by colleagues and false claims could be dealt with. Airmen who had seized the opportunity to promote themselves to officer rank were dealt with sympathetically and sent to join their companions. Far more serious were the fifth columnists who had managed to infiltrate our ranks and who might have presented a security threat had they not been singled out and whisked away to be locked up where they could do no harm. There was no place for them on Malta and I never knew what happened to them when we reached Marseilles. During the week that followed we sat as in a golden cage, showered with every comfort, enjoying sumptuous meals, smoking good English cigarettes, playing cards, talking and trying to acclimatise somehow to our new situation. We had everything but our liberty for we were not allowed off the ship and armed marines guarded the only gangway to make sure that none of us tried to go.

Eventually we sailed from Malta escorted by a destroyer. Once we reached the open sea we began again to experience the might of the waves. Even this large boat was tossed up and down and from side to side, and there were times when the escorting destroyer disappeared altogether as it plunged into a trough.

We sailed in zig-zags with no lights showing and these precautions amongst others brought it home to us that though we might have thought the war — our war — was already over and lost, here perhaps in the West the most serious stage was only just beginning. What was more, we were sailing not to escape but to play our part in whatever capacity we could.

There was comfort in that realisation.

18th NOVEMBER 1939
S.S. FRANCONIA

My dearest Zosia,

At last, after two months of wandering to escape the police of King Carol the First, I am beginning to feel that I am a person again and not a refugee. I am able at last to write to you telling you not only what has happened to me since we said goodbye but sharing with you my innermost feelings hoping and believing that you will understand. How and when these pages will reach you I don't know but surely one day a way will be found. Then, my little one, you will know the terrible pain that is in my heart because we are no longer together and the anguish of longing for you which is always with me.

Zosia, my dearest, you were and are everything to me. We had made such wonderful plans to be together for always in a dream world of our own. Now war has shattered that dream and we cannot tell what the future has in store for us. We must submit ourselves to God's will and cling to the hope that one day if we survive by some miracle — I fighting in a far-away land and you in the hell of war-torn Warsaw — we will still love each other and be together again.

Do you remember, my dearest, with what excitement and enthusiasm I used to talk about war? About fights in the sky and thrilling victories? I had fulfilled my ambition to train as a pilot and could hardly wait to play my full part. Even though it meant leaving you for a short while as I thought the pain of parting was balanced by happiness.

Now reality has caught up with me and I know how utterly wrong I was to glory in the thought of war, to take such a delight in it.

But this was not war as I had imagined it would be. It was disaster. One day it may be established with whom or with what lay the blame but for the moment we can only try to do all that is possible under these circumstances and be ready if such is our fate to die on the battlefield.

19th NOVEMBER 1939

At dawn after five days at sea we sailed into Marseilles and were read special orders from our General Sikorski welcoming us to France. Our spirits rose as we began to feel like fighting men again hoping soon to engage the enemy.

We were loaded into trains and after a whole night's journey arrived in Lyons where we were taken by lorries to the aerodrome. I was positively shaking with happiness to see the great silhouettes of hangars and the little roads crossing the airfield and to hear the so-familiar sound of engines. In a few days, I thought, I would be flying again.

How horribly mistaken I was! We were quartered not on the aerodrome but in a big exhibition hall nearby and I felt I was back in my initial training year as we slept on the floor on straw palliasses with just a couple of rough blankets to keep out the cold.

What was different was that instead of every minute of our days being occupied with duties performed at the double, there was literally nothing to do. Any form of real organisation was missing as had been the case all along. Polish senior officers created the familiar chaos as they issued a thousand commands and counter-commands and we had nothing to do but "rest after the hard times we had endured". We were so frustrated that we were ready to mutiny but there was little we could do in a foreign country. I wrote letters to you, my darling, and to my family but I was beginning to lose hope that they would ever reach you. In my despair I turned again to the only antidote I knew — drink. It did little to help and only made me feel more demoralised and disgusted with myself.

Christmas arrived, and it was time for Wigilia. It had always been such a very special day for us all with its traditions and ceremonies, its bringing together of all those we loved in commemoration of the birth of the Holy Child. Now we were spending it far from home and memories of other years were as painful to bear as were the fears as to how and where you would be spending it this year and even if you would still be alive to celebrate. We were allowed to use the Officers Mess at the aerodrome and somehow or other made an attempt at preparing the traditional dishes and singing our carols.

On Christmas Day I went for a long walk by myself, unable to bear the company of anyone. Somehow I came to the old cathedral on the banks of the Rhone and instinct took me inside. Mass was being celebrated and suddenly, magically, I was at home again as the familiar Latin phrases filled my ears and the music warmed my heart. I was alone and yet not alone and when Mass was over I stayed behind and slipped into one of the confessional boxes. The priest was French and my knowledge of the French language was by no means perfect particularly under so much emotional stress. However, he told me kindly to make my confession in Polish and I poured out to God all my fears, my failings, my frustrations. The absolution seemed to lift the enormous burden weighing me down and I felt a wonderful peace stealing through my veins as my belief in God's mercy was rekindled.

The remainder of our squadron joined us from Paris bringing with them the hope that any day now we would start to fly again. Best of all, we received letters from home including a letter and a photo from you, Zosia my dearest. It was almost like seeing you again and the letter was read over and over again until it was almost threadbare. The photo had been a little crumpled but no matter, it was like holding a part of you again. You and all I loved were alive and well. I thanked God with all my heart.

8th MARCH 1940
Winter was slowly giving way to Spring. Our conditions were improving at the same time. We were now issued with the dark blue uniforms of the French Air Force which in the need for equipping so many were made of coarse material but which at least made us feel that we belonged somewhere again and were no longer homeless refugees.

We were paid, too, and were able to leave the primitive conditions of the exhibition hall and find our own accommodation in Lyons. Six of us rented a large studio flat and I was nominated as cook with the task of providing acceptable meals from the food which was still in plentiful supply. Life was at least bearable and it was hurtful to think of you, Zosia, still suffering from cold and hunger and who knew what other privations.

Our duties were still minimal but at last it was decided that as pilots we should be given the chance to fly again. Knowing we were experienced pilots we were given somewhat sketchy information as to the essential differences between the aircraft which we had been used to flying and the French aircraft which we would be flying now. These were much more modern and involved learning about variable pitch and retractable under-carriages besides the unfamiliar instruments and armaments.

At last — at long last — at 2.20 pm on 8th March — I took to the skies again!

Our first aircraft were small civilian aircraft which had been requisitioned but at least they had been given Polish markings. We were led by Sergeant Beda and the sheer joy and relief of being airborne again was like that which must be felt by caged birds suddenly finding freedom.

After a few familiarisation flights we moved onto actual fighter aircraft — Corons and Marans — flying from a small airfield near the main aerodrome. Our role, we were told, was in the defence of St Etiennes and other industrial towns as well as of Lyons but there was little effective part for us to play. We saw German aircraft but with no radar or other advance warning of their approach besides their superior speed they had vanished before we could catch up with them.

Some of our pilots were killed trying to handle unfamiliar aircraft which were faster and more advanced than those we had known. Amongst them was my friend, Witek Dobrzynski. We buried him in friendly French soil. Tomorrow it may be my turn.

More letters were coming through and much as I loved hearing from you, my darling, my longing for you and uncertainty as to your fate were hard to bear. The Germans were taking thousands of our girls to labour camps in Germany. Others were being taken to brothels for the use of German troops. I can only ask God to protect you, my future wife, and to grant that I may find you again when the evil that has overtaken the world is finally defeated.

That defeat seems to be a long way away. We have heard that with the subjugation of Poland the Germans are turning their attention to Norway and the Low Countries.

10th MAY 1940
About 5.30 am I was awakened by the sound of anti-aircraft batteries.

Alert!

I made my way as quickly as I could to the aerodrome and found a scene of complete devastation. The Germans had made a direct bombing attack catching the French completely by surprise. Hangars, aircraft and buildings had been destroyed and eighteen ground crew had been killed — eight of them French and ten Polish. They had died for nothing without even the chance to fight back.

Everyone seemed to be in a maze of shock and despair that amounted almost to panic. France might officially be at war with Germany but it appeared that no one here actually believed it and life had gone on pretty much as normal.

At lunchtime there was a second attack and, although no one was killed, many were seriously wounded.

News came that Belgium and Holland had been over-run and that the Germans had incredibly taken over the front units of the Maginot Line itself. That was perhaps the most bitter blow of all. Everyone had put their faith in the Maginot Line as an impregnable defence against attack and now that faith was shattered.

We had been aware of covert remarks sometimes amounting to sneers that Poland had only been able to hold out for twenty-one days. Now other countries had fallen within forty-eight hours and the general attitude towards us warmed to something like respect. We must after all have fought to the bitter end and our pilots and ground crew were no longer outsiders relegated to less important roles but much-needed and welcome allies. What we had done for Poland we could now do for France and our skills and fighting experience would surely help to turn the tide running so remorselessly against the West. Some form of optimism returned. People spoke of "the beginning of the end". The crazy man from Berlin had surely over-reached himself and would soon get his deserts.

Frustrating days lay ahead. We were now based on the secondary airfield at Boron and resumed our training on aircraft which were not very modern but good compared with those we had flown in Poland.

We longed to get back into the fight and there were times when we envied those Polish squadrons who had preceded us to France, been destined for Finland, and then diverted to the Western front. News reached us of their victories and their sacrifices.

At least our squadron was now together in one group. We were supposed to be defending Lyons and were at readiness but there were no opportunities to engage the enemy. We had no advance warning of approaching German aircraft and although we took off as soon as they were spotted we were always too late and with our slower aircraft could not hope to catch up with them before they had vanished from sight.

1st JUNE 1940

We were supposed to be going at last to the front and grew disheartened when again we were reduced to waiting. Today there was another bombing of Lyons and at least those who took off first had the opportunity to fight. They were outnumbered nine to one but gave a good account of themselves. My great friend, Raymond Klapas, managed to shoot down a German aircraft but was shot down and killed.

By the time we arrived, it was all over.

2nd JUNE 1940
At last we were moved by lorry to an airfield near Sedan where the Germans were trying to cross the Marne. The whole Polish Wing was together and we were soon involved in a fierce battle. We were under the direction of a French officer — a Wing Commander — who did his best to deploy us to good advantage despite the superior numbers and superior aircraft of the Germans. If only his colleagues had been equally committed to the cause. In the midst of the general melee he spotted a whole wing of French aircraft some height above us and radioed them to come down and join us. The answer which we were beginning to recognise as typical of our "gallant allies' was that such a move was not included in the orders they had received.

I managed to chase some Germans but my specific task was to form some sort of defence for a group of British Fairy Battles who were bombing bridges across the Marne in an attempt to halt the enemy advance and my priority lay with them.

The next day we had orders from Polish H.Q. to move by train to Bordeaux. We arrived to find the usual mix-up with nothing really organised, nothing for us to do. In our frustration a group of us decided to award ourselves a welcome break and visit Paris.

Paris! It was quite uncanny. The news from all the war fronts was bad, the future grim, but as far as the people of Paris were concerned everything was normal. We just couldn't believe it — shops, restaurants, theatres and the lot were functioning as if the war was nothing but a bad dream from which they expected any moment to awake. It was a very long time since we had had the chance to enjoy a few carefree moments and we caught the prevailing mood.

The contrast with reality was almost too much for us and a kind of hysterical gaiety gripped us as we sat in a brightly-lit restaurant eating and drinking and observing the well dressed people around us. We went rather further than observing, in fact. A pretty woman with a small girl sat at a table nearby and we outdid each other in the exchange of bawdy remarks as to what we would like to do with her. She and the little girl rose to go and we were horrified to hear the little girl ask in perfect Polish:

"Mummy, are those gentlemen Poles?"

Her mother's eyes flashed fire at us and there was icy contempt in her voice as she said:

"No, darling, they are not Polish gentlemen — they are swine!"

It was a well-merited rebuke and we all felt thoroughly ashamed of ourselves. Perhaps, however, she might not have been quite as caustic had she known what we had all been through during the past dreadful months when there had been no light relief.

The only slight indication that some Parisians were more aware of what was happening than was made apparent was in the smell of burning paper everywhere which told of documents being destroyed before the inevitable arrival of the Germans.

4th JUNE 1940

We were not to stay in Bordeaux after all but move to La Rochelle for defence patrols of the coast. We eventually arrived. It was a beautiful coastline but we were not really in the frame of mind to appreciate it. Aircraft arrived for us to fly — Bloch, Moran — and we flew on patrol without seeing any of the enemy. We realised that they had been otherwise engaged when we heard the staggering news that the British expeditionary force were being evacuated from the Dunkirk beaches together with numbers of French and Belgian troops.

The Germans had bombed Paris killing forty-five people. It seemed incredible that only a couple of days before we had enjoyed our brief visit there when everything had seemed normal. What was happening to the world as we knew it? I felt completely dry of feeling. Nothing would surprise me any more.

I only awaited the chance to fight so that I could return home.

15th JUNE 1940

Yesterday the Germans entered Paris which was completely undefended. The French High Command saw no reason why it should not be handed over and the Germans marched in. The roads to the South were blocked with civilians who were continually dive-bombed.

In some respects it was like our flight to Romania but there was one essential difference — we had been caught between the advancing Germans and the Bolsheviks and retreated only to regroup and take up the fight again. The French government had fled to Tours some days previously and then on to Bordeaux where they were concerned only with how quickly they could give up the fight. They were utterly demoralised by the failure of the Maginot Line to protect them and had lost all will to fight even if it had ever existed. We heard that they were planning to sign an armistice.

The situation was indeed desperate for us. The Germans, we were told, were demanding that the French should hand us over to them for internment or maybe worse. Escape was imperative, but how?

I don't think any of us even considered the option of flying off in the aircraft still at our disposal. Our airmen were as much part of the squadron as we were. We had been together through all that had happened and must stay together.

Some friends flew in from other airfields. We must go to Bordeaux and then by some means or other get to England where we could continue to fight.

16th JUNE 1940

A group of us went to La Palisse. We had heard that they had managed to take off some English forces from there but that a lot of equipment had been left behind. Our immediate priority was to get lorries to take us to Bordeaux.

There were plenty of vehicles but the British had not intended them to fall into German hands and had made them unserviceable. Eventually we found one which by same miracle was undamaged and even had the ignition key in place. We lifted the cover and saw boxes labelled in a strange language which meant nothing to us and began to throw them unceremoniously from the lorry so that we would have room for the food which others from our group had salvaged from the other vehicles.

What a shock we got! One of the boxes we were so busy tossing aside burst open and we saw that it was full of live ammunition. We made a hasty momentary escape but when nothing terrible had happened returned and this time handled the boxes with kid gloves.

Another change of orders — we were not to go to Bordeaux but to Rochefort which was to be the assembly point for Polish troops whilst Polish aircraft maintained air cover. We took the coastal road which was jammed with refugees on foot and in all kinds of transport all heading West. There were a number of French troops who were thoroughly demoralised and needed no persuasion to exchange their arms for bottles of wine. We managed to reach Rochefort where not only Polish airmen but Polish Army troops complete with tanks and weapons were continuously arriving.

What a great joy it was to meet up with Colonel Pawlikowski. As had happened in Poland he was managing somehow to bring order out of chaos and to bring the scattered units into a cohesive band. I had such confidence in him that I was able to calm some of my bewilderment amounting almost to despair and to feel that all would somehow be well.

17th JUNE 1940

In the morning a group of twelve lorries and some two hundred and fifty men were ordered to La Rochelle where, we were told, we would transfer to a small French boat called *Rouen*.

The *Rouen* was there but the Port Commandant refused to let us board. He insisted that his orders were to hand us over to the Germans.

A few hours went by whilst Colonel Pawlikowski tried his best to negotiate at the Port Headquarters. We were becoming more and more desperate as we surrounded the Headquarters, putting on a show of strength which we hoped might prove effective when persuasion and appeals to treat allies as allies and not as enemies had failed. It was a stalemate situation and time was obviously not on our side as the Germans were already in Breste and Nantes. And then — salvation!

A young Lieutenant from the Royal Navy resplendent in white uniform and accompanied by six Marines arrived at the Headquarters and in perfect French informed the Port Commandant that he had orders to load us on the *Aderpool*, a collier returning from Malta, which was on its way. The Port Commandant was shaking with fury, insisting that he would obey orders and keep us until the Germans arrived. If necessary he would enforce those orders with the battery of 45 mm guns which were in place on the Ile de Re just offshore. This threat did not cause the Royal Navy Lieutenant to waver for an instant. He quietly stated that his destroyer was equipped with far heavier guns than the French could produce and that he would not hesitate to use them if necessary against an ally who had suddenly became a traitor. Then — a master-stroke — he offered to provide a document proving that the Port Commandant had only disobeyed under extreme duress, an offer which the Frenchman welcomed and accepted.

Towards evening the *Aderpool* tied up at the end of the long mole and we were told to start embarkation together with remnants of infantry.

18th JUNE 1940

There were a few women members of the Polish and French forces and the Captain ordered them to move to the crew's quarters where they would have toilets, cooking facilities and privacy.

The rest of us clambered down iron ladders onto temporary decks formed from what had been the hold for coal. It was for all the world like packing eggs for as soon as one level was full a timber floor was laid on top ready for the next consignment of troops. We were lucky enough to have accommodation on the top deck thanks to Squadron-Leader Frey. As the night progressed we could hear the whistling sound of dive bombers and explosion of bombs as the *Rouen* and the whole area of dockland came under attack. The poor little boat on which we had planned originally to sail was a mass of flames. It seemed to us evidence of the existence of a Fifth Column active in the area for otherwise why should it have been singled out for attention?

Every half hour or so other bombers arrived to make their contribution

Polish servicemen crowded into the Aderpool — *a converted British collier — which carried Tadeusz from La Rochelle to Plymouth.*

to the fires and the emergency services were quite unable to cope. During all this time the queue continued to wind its way up the mole onto the *Aderpool*. We felt like sitting ducks on board, scarcely daring to breathe let alone show a light in case we drew attention to ourselves. Had the Germans struck no one could have survived but somehow fear was replaced by resignation to our fate. We had endured so much and there was nothing we could do now except pray. Towards dawn we saw a moving light in the sun above the horizon. The embarkation was complete and we had started to move out from our moorings. As the light came nearer we saw that it was a Heinkel III going towards the fires. It flew over us and seeing our loaded boat turned to dive on us.

All our anti-aircraft machine guns which we had taken on board with us suddenly acquired a vital significance. We opened fire with everything that we had sending out thousands of different coloured tracers. The Heinkel swerved sharply, dropping its bombs harmlessly away from us and disappeared. The emergency was over for the moment and we sailed on towards the open sea.

10th JULY 1940

We have arrived in England and are at Blackpool, a holiday resort on the west coast.

It was a long and complicated journey especially as for some time we did not know where we were going. The *Aderpool* had none of the comforts of the *Franconia*, just a few feet of deck on which I crouched and tried to make myself as small as possible which was stupid because crowded as we were an attack from the air or from a submarine would have sent us all to the bottom of the ocean. The only toilets were in the crew's quarters occupied by the women sailing with us and it was a case of balancing on the ship's rails whilst colleagues grasped our legs.

However, we had water and were well supplied with the two priorities for any Pole — food and arms. We had clung onto those stocks through all that had happened. The main thing was we had avoided being handed over to the Germans and we were so relieved that we were almost light-hearted. One youngster even had an accordion with him which he played to add to the atmosphere.

We sailed due west at first and wondered briefly if we were going to Canada but then turned east and on the morning of the third day reached a port which we gathered was Plymouth.

It was pouring with rain — we had always known that it rained all the time in England — but our welcome was warm and friendly even if we could not understand a word that was said. As we disembarked ladies in green overalls handed each of us a mug of hot tea and some sandwiches. We were soon to find that English tea is quite different from our pale lemon-tasting Polish tea. It is very strong and bitter, dark brown in colour, and was thick with milk and sugar. However it was the first hot drink we had had for days and we were glad of it. The sandwiches contained a thin filling of a peculiar pink spread which we found later to be fish paste — we were not hungry enough to take more than an experimental bite and threw them discreetly away. We were at once impressed by the English powers of organisation. There was no waiting around, no chaos. We were loaded immediately into trains and off we went.

Two or three times we pulled into a station to be given more tea and fish paste sandwiches and eventually reached a city which turned out to be Glasgow where we were taken just outside and housed in the buildings of a large university called Strathclyde. We stayed there for three days and were well treated with plenty of fresh food although we had to sleep on the floor on piles of fresh straw. It was like a return to the early days of my training.

On the fourth day we were taken by lorry to a large multi-story building in Glasgow which had been vacated for us and the staircase which led up to it from the floor below had been fenced off with a rope to keep the public away. Whoever had thought of that had misjudged the Scottish shoppers who were curious and large numbers of whom came to peer over the rope. What a shock they had to see naked or half-naked men making full use of facilities to wash and shave not to mention the sight of machine guns and other arms in piles. It was no wonder they screamed and beat a hasty retreat.

Two days later we went by train to West Kirby, a training camp for overseas forces which was still under construction. Despite the work still to be done it was already as comfortable as permanent camps in Poland and France with washing facilities, hot water, electricity and even paths leading from one area to another. Here we met up with colleagues who had arrived in England by various routes and basked in the smiling, obviously admiring faces of English people looking at us over the perimeter fencing. We might have worn uniforms which were dirty and decidedly past their best but at least we were recognised as sturdy welcome allies.

After a few days we were on the move by train again and found ourselves at Blackpool. It reminded us slightly of Paris with its big tower dominating the town but were sure that would be the end of the resemblance — we were now in England, not France, and a new phase of our lives was to begin.

A row of English policemen were there at the station and once we had been divided into groups they led us to the Promenade where there were long rows of houses. Our particular policeman halted us outside one house, knocked at the door and told the woman who answered it that we were her appointed guests.

Poor Mrs. Leach! We discovered that to be the name of our landlady. In common with the owners of other boarding-houses and small private hotels along the Promenade, she had been appointed as part of her war duties to give homes to the Polish forces crowding the town.

At first no doubt she had been glad of the opportunity to earn a regular income filling rooms no longer required for holiday-makers but the dismay on her face when she first saw what she had let herself in for showed that she was already regretting it. And who could blame her? Shabby, armed to the teeth, unable to speak a word of English, how could she cope with us?

Gritting her teeth she let us in and we were shown to the rooms which were to be our home for the foreseeable future. They were by no means big rooms and as many beds as possible had been crammed into them, but at least they were real beds and we were in no mood to be critical. Hardly had we selected our beds than a gong sounded and we were led into the dining-room for a meal which we were to know as high tea, a custom dear to English people whose status and income did not allow for evening dinner. We were hungry — when are Poles not hungry? — and our spirits fell when we took in the plates containing a sparse salad plus a very thin piece of tinned ham supplemented by piles of bread and butter and a dish containing one cake each of a type we had never seen before. Was this to be the full extent of our diet in the future, we wondered? England was certainly a strange country in which we had found ourselves.

28th AUGUST 1940

It is Mamusia's name day and for the first time ever I can't even send her a card let alone hug her and kiss her and celebrate with her. I am entirely cut off from her just as I am from you, Zosia my dearest, and from all those I hold dear.

I am sunk in apathy and despair and haven't been able even to write my feelings down. All I want is to get back in the air where I belong and play my part in ending this dreadful war which is ruining so many people's lives. It begins to look as though that is not to be, that I am doomed to sit around here whilst my friends from the Lafayette squadron have already gone to train.

All my hopes were dashed soon after I arrived in Blackpool. It was not enough that all the arms we had brought with us to England were taken from us to be distributed to the Free French, far worse was to come as far as I was concerned.

We were all taken for medical examinations which we thought would be a mere formality. We were fit and healthy and had already passed so many rigorous medicals. That turned out to be true as far as the others were concerned but I was rejected.

I found it hard to believe — I still cannot believe or accept it. The English medical examiner told me that my eyesight was too bad to pass for flying — that I had a squint which would lead me to break up any aircraft on landing. I did my best to protest. Through the interpreter I told him of the hours I had flown in Poland and in France, the air battles I had fought, the many different types of aircraft I had handled, the fact that I had not only flown myself but had instructed other pilots in flying. It was useless. He only became angry and said that his decision was final.

Can you even begin to imagine my reactions, Zosia darling? Never to be allowed to fly when it was all I had trained so hard for, proved a success at, and relied on to give a purpose to my life and atone for all that I and others had been through? I spent so much time pestering our high-ranking Polish Officers in Blackpool, urging them to do something to get the mistake recognised, but they just did not want to know. They were too busy enjoying their good conditions, their status to have time for me. One or two of them even expressed surprise that I should want to risk my life in the air when I had such a good excuse to enjoy safe and comfortable living.

And then, by a miracle, I met up with Colonel Pawlikowski who proved once again to be worthy of all the trust and respect I have always held for him. He at least understood how I felt and told me that he had no intention of being deprived of one of his experienced and valued pilots because of a silly mistake. He said he would pull all the strings he could to get me another medical at the Air Ministry.

If only, only he can do this my troubles will be over.

8th SEPTEMBER 1940

My trust in Colonel Pawlikowski was not misplaced. Yesterday I was sent by train with an interpreter to London, to the Air Ministry, to another medical this time with an Air Commodore who specialised in eye conditions.

It was so completely different. He spoke French quite well so we were able to communicate and the interpreter was there to fill in any gaps. It was an exhaustive test and included elements that were new to me. In one of them I had to look through a sort of peephole at a tiger made from pipe cleaners which I had to put into a cage. At the end of it he pronounced me absolutely fit to fly, shook my hand, and wished me luck. It was as though a huge black cloud had rolled away from me and for the first time for many weary weeks there was hope in my heart.

The interpreter had his family in London and when he asked me if he could go and see them for a brief visit before meeting me at Euston on the train for Blackpool, I assured him that I would manage perfectly.

I was glad of the opportunity to see something of London. After all, I had been born and brought up in Warsaw, our own capital city, and had coped very well in Paris so had no reason to lack confidence in my ability to get around.

What I had not taken into account, of course, was that I could speak hardly a word of English and passers-by that I approached could not understand French let alone Polish. My wanderings had left me completely lost with no idea which direction I should take in order to reach Euston.

There was a policeman on point duty at a busy road crossing and I had already discovered that here in Britain the Police were there to help people in trouble. I made my way over to him and managed to attract his attention. I showed him my warrant and managed to stammer out:

"Me Pole. Euston. Blackpool."

He did not bat an eyelid. Halting the traffic, he took me to the nearest bus stop, put me onto a bus, and explained to the conductress my predicament. Of course I did not understand what he said but she did which was the main thing. She sat me down in a seat with a reassuring smile and pat on the shoulder and I was on my way. Several stops later she rang the bell twice for the driver to wait, led me by the hand to another bus, explained matters to a second conductress who was equally friendly, and waved me goodbye. It seemed like a miracle when we stopped outside the station whose portico I recognised. The ticket collector at the barrier read my warrant and escorted me to a train already standing at a platform. I was so thankful to be safely in my corner seat and was determined not to move again without my interpreter who would surely find me before the train left.

What no one could have foreseen was that the Germans should have

73

chosen that precise time to launch their first major attack on London. The eerie sound of sirens set my heart thumping as people left the train to join others on the platform scurrying to the shelters. I was urged to go along with them but nothing on earth would have induced me to move. I could hear bombs dropping and the deafening sound of anti-aircraft guns but I was more frightened of missing my train than of being killed. Somehow I knew that Hitler would not get me on the ground — my battle with him was in the sky.

Eventually the All Clear went, the station began to return to normal, and an extremely worried interpreter found me having searched the full length of the train.

We had time for the familiar cup of tea and fish paste sandwiches before the train was ready to leave and for once I welcomed them. I was tired, hungry and thirsty after my adventures and furthermore my weeks with Mrs. Leach had dulled my palate into submission.

The train filled up with passengers and eventually pulled out of the station but we did not seem to have travelled far when the bombers returned and we were forced to halt on an embankment high above streets and houses where we could actually see bombs exploding and fires starting.

There was an elderly English couple in our compartment. He stood looking out of the window and beckoned his wife to come and stand beside him. The interpreter told me that his words to her, spoken so calmly, were:

"Come and watch, my dear. This is probably something which you will never have the chance to see again."

I truly marvelled and for the first time actually believed in my heart that the British were a people whom it would take far, far more than Hitler to defeat. It was so clear that this was their belief.

14th FEBRUARY 1941
I am so fed up that I have not even been able to write in my diary. What is there to say but to record the same routine day after day with the chance of getting back into flying still no nearer.

Once the problem of my eyesight had been sorted out and I was passed fit I thought it would only be a matter of days before I was back where I belonged, where I wanted so much to be. Colonel Pawlikowski has assured me he has put me back in 303 Squadron, it is just a case of waiting for my posting to come through.

The trouble is that the squadrons are already fully made up. So many of our people came to England by a different route long before we did and were already trained and ready to fight. Now they are fighting, playing their full part in the defence of Britain, proving their value to the allied cause. Many of them are stationed at Northolt defending London which has had to endure heavy and concentrated bombing night after night. I feel so proud when I hear what they have done and are doing — they have destroyed 120 German aircraft with very few losses to themselves and the British people no longer think of them as 'Polish Travellers' but as a valued and integrated part of the forces. Two of my friends from 303 came to see me and have promised they will do all that they can to see that Tadek Kratko and I join them once again.

Have I mentioned Kratko to you, Zosia? If not it is perhaps that I am so familiar with him that I take him for granted. He was with me in the Squadron and we came to Blackpool and to Mrs. Leach's together. Together we share the monotony of our days when we have nothing to do but attend English classes (I shall never speak the language properly) and so-called training sessions which are a repeat of what we learned in our second year when we had not even flown. We also do P.T. on the beach with all types of servicemen and are always secretly amused by the rugged, sturdy structure of Poles compared with people of other nationalities.

We fill our time as best we can but it is difficult when we are given only seventeen English shillings a week to spend on things other than food and lodging which is provided.

One day I met two Polish sailors from a trawler at Fleetwood near Blackpool and they were delighted to hear that I knew how to handle weapons and said how valuable I would be in protecting their trawler. I took a tram to Fleetwood and met their skipper who was more than ready to welcome me aboard and said he would apply to get me transferred from the Air Force as at least with them I would be contributing to the war effort. I might have known that it was not to be. Permission was refused. I was a regular officer of the Polish Air Force and as such must do what the powers-that-be ordered even if it meant kicking my heels in idleness at Blackpool.

Kratko and I managed to find something to interest us. On one of our wanderings we saw a car in the grounds of a house. Did I say car? It had once been a car but was now used to house the owner's hens. On an impulse we went to look at it and spoke to the owner, asking if he would sell it to us. He laughed but said we could have it for £10 if we wanted it and could get it to start. Between us we managed to scrape together the money. We had no petrol but using lighter fuel managed to get it to start which it did first time. We then towed it back to Mrs. Leach's and were able to work on it in her back yard. It was soon able to be driven and gave us a new sense of freedom. We called it 'Little Stable' because it was no longer a henhouse but a genuine car even if it did date from 1927 and had seen better days.

One joy was that at last we were fitted with our Royal Air Force officers' uniforms in which we felt very smart and no longer bedraggled refugees. Unfortunately no posting came to go with the uniforms or — worst of all — came and proved false. We were so delighted as we presented ourselves at the station only to find that there had been a mistake which, we were told, was the fault of the Polish Administration. It was the all-too-familiar story — chaos and confusion and our protests as we went from one desk to another were of no avail.

Christmas was coming, and we decided to go and spend it with colleagues in 302 squadron who were based at Leconfield in Yorkshire. We also decided that we would travel in Little Stable as it was only from the west coast to the east coast and England was a small country. It was a good deal further than we had thought and we had to coax and even bully Little Stable along but eventually we arrived.

There was plenty to eat, plenty to drink, and a lot of hilarious conversation. Perhaps we were all making a conscious effort as we celebrated Wigilia and the rest of Christmas, remembering those other Christmases we had spent in our our country with those we loved. We helped each other and the flowing vodka helped too and we were feeling quite cheered as after four days we took the road back to Blackpool.

On the way we called in at a pub and met a group of men driving an empty hearse which was parked outside. They too were full of the Christmas spirit and listened with interest to our plan that we should swap their hearse for Little Stable. Unfortunately when one of them went to check the deal with his boss on the telephone the jollity ended abruptly. They were ordered to return immediately with the hearse and we resumed our journey to Blackpool.

Surely our waiting was nearly over?

How mistaken we were. It is now mid-February and the weeks still drag by. Will our enforced patience ever be rewarded?

4th MARCH 1941
At last! At last! Our call-up papers have arrived. We were told to go to the Central Flying Station at Upavon, near Salisbury. We could hardly believe it.

We decided to drive there in Little Stable which was not as easy as it sounds. We were hopelessly lost in Manchester but calling in at a pub to refresh our spirits were lucky enough to meet up with an off-duty fireman who told us to follow his car and we were soon safely on our way. Who said the English were a cold unfriendly race with a dislike for foreigners?

We arrived safely at Upavon and reported as told to the English

Squadron Leader. He was friendly and welcoming but he looked so absurdly young. Maybe he was only a year or so younger than we were in actual years but the experiences we had gone through had made us old before our time. This came over particularly when he asked me how many flying hours I had done and laughed rather shamefacedly when I told him it was just over three thousand — his total, he admitted, was two hundred and eighty.

Nevertheless it was his job to make sure that we were trained and able to fly and I at any rate had to admit that it was necessary.

The Tudors and Masters aircraft were new to me and quite frankly my flying skills were a little rusty after nearly nine months confined unwillingly to the ground.

Nine months! Can you imagine, Zosia, how I felt to be back in the air? It was like being released from a long prison sentence and I felt free again as my confidence returned.

There were other Polish pilots on the station together with some New Zealanders who were also a long way from home. Evenings in the Mess were devoted to a kind of false gaiety as we drank ourselves legless and sang Polish songs to the accompaniment of a piano played more with determination than with musical ability.

Once or twice a group would pile into Little Stable and we would drive into Salisbury in search of further entertainment. Again local people were kind to us and turned a blind eye to our noisy exuberance. I remember once starting up the engine to return to Upavon and coming to a grinding halt. A torch shone in our faces and we were addressed by a genial Special Constable who asked where we were going. We assured him that we knew the way but he shook his head and said that we were wedged against the garden wall of a house. However, if we turned right and went over the railway crossing we would be on the road to Upavon. He said he had been watching us and as we were travelling at little over walking pace he thought we would eventually get there without mishap.

23rd MARCH 1941

We were on the move again. We were to report to a different training school at Acklington, north of Newcastle. Again our valiant Little Stable took us on our journey north of some three hundred and fifteen miles.

We were to join 317 Squadron which for some reason was known as the Wilno Squadron although there was only one pilot from Wilno.

It all seemed very strange and we knew none of the other pilots. However, we were progressing from flying training aircraft to actual fighters, Hurricane Mark One, and that seemed to be a step in the right direction.

29th MARCH 1941

New orders! After less than a week we were to go to Sutton Bridge for more training. This time we travelled two hundred and forty miles South-East. We were certainly having a round tour of Britain but were finding it harder and harder to appreciate it.

8th APRIL 1941

They couldn't seem to decide what to do with us! Orders came for us to return to Acklington and rejoin 317 Squadron. If we were getting more than a little tired of so many seemingly pointless changes, poor Little Stable was in her death throes. It was a nightmare journey. The tyres blew. The engine smelled. We had to use all our ingenuity and mechanical ability to coax her along knowing with sad hearts that this would be the last time she would take us on our travels. At least back at Acklington we became a real part of the Squadron and were put on operations.

Our task was to patrol convoys along the coast from the Tyne to the Firth of Forth. We never saw a German, but were constantly in peril from the guns of the ships we were there to protect. We had coloured signal rockets so that the ships could identify us but they seemed to have decided to be safe rather than sorry and opened fire. We had to fly very low over them so that they could see the recognition marks below our wings before they could be induced to accept our support and this made life hazardous. The coast was rocky and unfriendly in the extreme and offered no opportunity for a forced landing if one should become necessary and there was little comfort to be gained from the idea of ditching in the grey heaving waters of the North Sea.

Carrying out convoy protection at night was even less pleasant although when on night patrol we flew from Ouston some fifteen miles from Acklington which struck me as being a more friendly station where we felt welcome.

6-7th MAY 1941

Last night the Germans arrived.

I was at Ouston on a spell of night-flying but was not on duty at the time. In consequence I spent the evening in the Mess forgetting my troubles in the way to which I had became all too accustomed — with the bottle.

I went outside, roused by the distinctive sound of enemy aircraft, and there they were. They had switched on their navigation lights and were clearly set for business. They dropped bombs on the hangar and strafed the airfield, by the grace of God missing the Naafi building where a dance was just finishing but creating plenty of havoc nevertheless. Three of our aircraft were destroyed and four damaged.

I could see one of them on fire and in my rage and bottle-courage I went over to it. I took off my coat as I went with the crazy idea of extinguishing the flames and was only saved from certain death from the exploding petrol tanks by the quick action of one of our ground crew who rushed after me and firmly took me out of harm's way.

Oh Zosia dearest, how sad you would be to see your 'hero' reduced to such a state of drunken folly! You would surely not be proud of me now — I was just as surely not proud of myself. But it seemed the only way I had of dealing with my separation from you and all that I loved and my utter frustration at being denied the chance to meet the hated Germans in my natural element, the air, where I could use all my skill and training to ensure their defeat or die in the attempt.

2nd JUNE 1941

On the move yet again! One way and another we are certainly getting to know a multitude of areas in Great Britain — England, Scotland and now Wales. Our new base is on an unfinished airfield on the Gower Peninsula and we are living in tents as the buildings are only half-completed. Not that that is any hardship. I am well used to such conditions after my years as a Scout and during initial training for the Forces as well as wartime spells in Poland and later in France. Creature comforts count for very little — all that matters is the chance to get into the air and fight the Germans in the only way I know.

We certainly have plenty of opportunity to be airborne now. 317 is a Reserve Squadron which means that we can be called upon to fly in any capacity for which we are needed. There is certainly plenty of variety even if dogfights with the enemy have not come my way. Once I enjoyed the fun and freedom of my grasshopper days, now I feel more like an ant following orders and plodding my way through job after job. At least I am never sure what the next day will bring. Sometimes it is back to convoy duties, this time protecting tankers who have crossed the Atlantic and are on their way to Milford Haven. From early dawn till dusk we take off in our Hurricanes, two at a time, flying across the grey wastes of the Irish Sea and the Bristol Channel to pick up the tankers. It is always essential to keep an eye on our fuel tanks so that we are not forced to ditch in the sea or make a forced landing on the rocky inhospitable coast. Fog and low clouds are a menace and there have been several accidents causing damage to aircraft and pilots. According to the location of the tankers we might go as far as the Irish coast — Eire being a neutral country it is strange to see the lights and life going on as normal. Sometimes our escort duties lead us right to Milford Haven where we circle in our protective role whilst the tankers unload.

The next day orders might come to fly to the south coast as escort to bombers crossing the English Channel to attack the coast anywhere between Cherburg and Ostend, Lille being the maximum. We have to fly cross-country to Dungeness, Selsey Bill or similar places where we refill our fuel tanks and wait for the Blenheims and 4-engined Stirlings setting off to 'drop their eggs' where they will hurt most. The times of take-off vary and we must wait at readiness in our cockpits sometimes for an hour at a time before the bombers are on their way.

The bombers do their job effectively but are slow and cumbersome and no match for modern German fighters. It is our job to provide a protective canopy which on occasion might be five layers in depth ranging from 15,000 to 30,000 feet. It is imperative that we should fly in close formation and we have strict orders that on no account must we break off on adventures of our own.

Flying Hurricanes, we form the lowest layer whilst the swift, more manoeuvrable Spitfires are way above us where the real action is. It is tantalising to hear on the intercom the shouts and other sounds of battle, particularly when Douglas Bader, Paddy Finucane and other famous air aces are notching up further victories.

Our battle is with the anti-aircraft fire which presents all too real a threat but which is nothing compared to the damage inflicted on the bombers. It is heart-breaking to see so many brought down into the fire and smoke from bombs which have landed and to know that the numbers we shall escort home will be far fewer than those on the outward flight. We have to circle and wait whilst their mission is completed and then do our best to shepherd the remnants, often badly-crippled, to the English coast.

We know we are doing essential work whatever our duties but you, Zosia my dearest, will understand how desperately hard it is to submit to the discipline imposed on us. After all our experiences when we played an active role it is terrible to be able to do so little. It is our Polish nature to be rash, impulsive — foolhardy even — and now yet again we must do the mundane duties whilst the excitement, the exhilaration, the do-or-die glory of battle falls to others.

29th JUNE 1941
We moved to Exeter to form part of the Polish Wing now based in Devon and Somerset. Our barracks were attached to an old country house on the

way to Honiton although quite often flying duties meant our landing at other air fields along the South Coast.

We were still playing much the same role — protecting shipping and escorting bombers to France. There were differences, of course, apart from the fact that it was now the English Channel over which we flew.

Instead of oil tankers coming and going to Milford Haven we were protecting shipping from major ports such as Plymouth. They had to sail close to the coast and I got to know the coastline pretty well with all its bays and promontories. Normally we handed over to other pilots based further west but quite often we had to go further and on many occasions had to land and refuel at Predannock in Cornwall. Yes, we were still flying Hurricanes which were not the speediest of aircraft. They had limited fuel capacity causing us always to keep an anxious eye on the fuel gauge so that we did not have to ditch in the sea or on some rocky height miles from anywhere such as happened to too many pilots with subsequent damage to themselves and their aircraft.

I can't say I enjoyed these duties although I knew that they had to be done but it all seemed very tame and monotonous compared with what I wanted so much to do. There were some interesting moments, of course, particularly the day when I spotted the submarine anchored almost on the coast. It was in comparatively shallow water and seemed quite undisturbed as I circled overhead, trying to decide if it was a British submarine which had perhaps been damaged or if it was actually a German U-Boat. I shall never know! I radioed in with its position and at my de-briefing on landing told the Intelligence Officer who said it should be reported but that was the last I heard of the matter.

The bombers we were now escorting across the Channel had a dangerous and difficult job indeed. Their bombs were for the busy, heavily-guarded ports of Brest, Cherbourg and Le Havre where the Germans had massed their shipping strength and their heaviest anti-aircraft weapons. The odds were stacked against them from the beginning and it tore your heart out to see so many shot down or so badly mauled that it took us all our time to stay with them as they limped home. Quite often the need to keep with them meant that our fuel was exhausted and we had to land with them and see at first hand waiting ambulances taking the dead and horribly injured out of aircraft so badly damaged that only a miracle could have brought them back.

I often thanked God that as a fighter pilot I flew alone, responsible only for myself and not for members of a crew. We were by no means clear of danger ourselves, of course, and had to take a good deal of evasive action to avoid the anti-aircraft barrage. We had small one-seater dinghies attached to our parachutes in case of trouble. If we had to bail out it was a case of opening the parachute and at exactly the right moment inflating the dinghy hoping that it would not become entangled with the parachute cords.

My friend Kratko had first-hand experience of this. He had to bail out in the choppy grey waters of the English Channel and although he radioed in his position it was some time before the rescue boat reached him. He had injured his heel and the perilous business of scrambling from his dinghy up to the boat did him no good at all. In fact he was taken to hospital and it was some time before he could discard his crutches and plaster and walk again. Another pilot — Flying Officer Karol Woicek — was less lucky. He was shot down and killed, the first loss suffered by 317 Squadron.

There was one addition to our duties. When not required as escorts we were put on readiness to drive off German aircraft flying in on nuisance raids anywhere along the South coast. This meant sitting in the cockpit waiting to hear that a 'bandit' had been spotted in a particular vector and then taking off in the hope of a fight at last. It was a pretty vain hope as our Hurricanes were little match for the Messerschmidts and Fokkers of the Luftwaffe. They had usually done their dirty deeds and vanished before we could reach them. However, on one glorious occasion the Squadron managed to shoot down two Messerschmidts which brought great joy to all of us even if I have to admit that I was more than a little envious not having had a share in the victory.

Nothing seemed to be going my way and as weeks became months I found myself becoming more and more despondent. I tried not to show it and joined in all the off-duty fun and games although I knew I was relying more and more on drink to get me into the right frame of mind.

Even in a crowd I felt so utterly alone.

I was with my fellow countrymen but not of them and it went deeper than the fact that almost all of them came from Wilno rather than from my beloved Warsaw. 317 had been the last Polish squadron to be formed and there was a wide gulf between the higher rank pilots who had been given the task of forming and running it and the junior ranks under their control. The senior officers had fought in British squadrons during the Battle of Britain, many of them with great gallantry, and rather naturally felt themselves to be a cut above the rest of us who had not shared their experiences. The junior officers were so much younger than I was — a generation younger in experience if not in years apart from Kratko who was still being treated for his injuries. They did not share my memories of those unforgettable times in the early days of the war.

Their whole attitude seemed to be different from mine. Either they felt with justice that they had done their bit and were now entitled to a quiet life or they were more than satisfied with the war as they were fighting it and had no ambition to taste of headier things.

One thing that horrified me was their lax approach to security. Having been a Technical Officer and knowing how vital a matter it was I found it hard to have my fears laughed at or totally ignored. On one occasion, probably fortified by alcohol, I held forth at length to one of our most senior officers and said I was ready to show him there and then what I meant. Probably because he too was in a drink-mellowed mood he accepted my bet of a bottle of whisky that I could get not only onto the airfield but up to the aircraft themselves without being challenged. We put on raincoats with no insignia, borrowed a small car which would not be recognised, and drove the few miles to the airfield. I was driving, and I pulled up at the main gates impressive enough with their brick guardhouse and uniformed guards. I let open the window.

"Everything all right, Sergeant ?" I said in my best broken English.

There was no attempt to check my credentials or those of my companion as we were waved through. That alerted my companion to the fact that there was definitely something in what I had been saying and he was all for jumping out and dealing with the matter there and then. I had not fully won my bet, however, and I persuaded him to go further. We drove right to the perimeter to where aircraft were parked. I got out of the car and whipped off one of the covers. There was no indication that anyone had so much as noticed us. I climbed into the aircraft and started up the engine — still no one took the slightest notice.

I won my bottle of whisky and after that security was certainly tightened up. I should have been satisfied but it seemed a hollow victory.

Just as I had made up my mind years previously that the time had come to leave the Grasshoppers in search of something more and had set about achieving it by any means I could, I was determined now to seek reparation for the long months of unfulfilled time at Blackpool and here in a squadron where I did not belong.

It is wrong to bear grudges but there were few days when I did not think hardly of the Medical Officer whose mistake over my eyesight had cost me my chance of joining up again with pilots who flew as I did, thought as I did, shared the attitudes and memories that I had.

Somehow or other I must hasten the day when we can all be together again but rack my brain as I might I cannot yet see my way to achieving it.

11th NOVEMBER 1941

This has been a truly memorable day.

Our President — our own Polish President — visited the Squadron. For the first time for such an age I felt not an alien in a foreign land but a Pole in a setting which had become however temporarily Poland. This was our Squadron, our airfield, and we had our rightful place here which we had earned.

The President had two reasons for coming. He was here to present decorations to those who had so richly deserved them by their gallantry

The extraordinary battle standard being handed by the Polish President to 317 Squadron on 11th November 1941.

under fire. One after another they stepped forward to receive their D.F.C. — The British Distinguished Flying Cross — which marked not just a tolerance of the Polish presence here but an appreciation of the contribution made. The second reason was even more dramatic. He handed over the Polish Air Force standard which we were to have the enormous privilege of keeping until it was handed over in turn to another squadron.

It was no ordinary standard, this. It had been worked in small pieces by devoted Polish women and smuggled to England to be joined up ready to fly in all its glory. They had literally risked their lives to produce it for had they been caught it would have meant the death penalty. We did not know their names and I suppose each of us wondered secretly if a wife, a mother, a sister or a girl friend had been involved in its production. I am sure I was not the only one to feel unshed tears stinging my eyes as we thought of their courage and the message it conveyed that though so far away their love for and pride in us remained unchanged.

Amongst the senior officers attending I was delighted to see my much-respected Colonel Pawlikowski. He had always been such a beacon of hope to me both in the early days in Poland and in rescuing me from durance vile in Blackpool when he had arranged for a fresh medical for me. Just to see him did me good and I could not believe my good fortune when mixing with us after the celebration lunch which followed the parade he actually recognised me. He did more than that. He came and talked to me and asked what I was doing and how felt about it. And knowing that this was a God-given chance, I told him. I told him of my frustrations, my despair, my longing to be in the front line, and although he was no longer my Commanding Officer he listened and understood. After all he had know me long enough and well enough to know how I chafed and fretted when things were not going my way and perhaps he had some sympathy for my fellow pilots as well as for me. He laid his hand briefly but kindly on my shoulder and promised to see what he could do to have me posted to 316 where my friends were.

Oh Zosia, hope has been reborn within me and the black cloud which has lain over me for so long at last has a silver lining. I can smile again.

25th DECEMBER 1941

Christmas was approaching again and we began to think about and plan for Wigilia. My third Wigilia spent away from you, Zosia mine, and from all those I loved. My heart was with you all and memories of wonderful times of warmth and love and laughter as we celebrated the age-old traditions were very much in my heart and mind.

Did all my colleagues feel the same sadness and longing for a home which might have been a million miles away so distant it was? I am sure that they did but each one hid his innermost feelings for the sake of the others and did his best to put on a brave face.

We were determined to celebrate in the best way we could and in this we were helped by our Intelligence Officer. He was English but spoke a little Polish and was a good friend to us all. He had married a Polish girl but she was away doing her duty in the F.A.N.Y. so rather than stay alone in his beautiful country house he had moved into our Mess.

Hearing us talk of Wigilia and wonder where we could manage to obtain the carp and pike and other fresh-water fish that we needed, he gave us permission to fish in the huge lakes running inland from the sea and forming part of his extensive grounds. With high hopes we took a couple of vans and those off-duty set off armed with pieces of old netting. Alas! Try as we might we had nothing to show for our efforts and finally decided to give up. One of our sergeants asked us to wait a moment as he had left some equipment on the lakeshore and a short time later we heard an unmistakable report. He had tossed a grenade into the water and when we rushed towards him we found almost more fish than we could take into our nets. Unethical? Of course it was but we did not stop to think of that as we returned in triumph with our bounty.

In the British forces it is the custom for officers to serve Christmas dinner to other ranks but we all celebrated our Wigilia together, rank forgotten, drinking our fill and singing Polish carols at the top of our voices. Far from home we might be but part of England had become Poland for the occasion and we laughed and joked even if tears lay behind our laughter.

14th MARCH 1942

Your Tadek is himself again! The black depression in which I had lived so long has lifted and there is no longer the need to pickle myself in alcohol just to get by.

I am at Heston, back with my friends and colleagues in 316 squadron which has been formed from the remains of our Owls and Swallows. I have now been promoted to Flying Officer and am flying a Spitfire Mark 5 armed with two canons and four machine guns.

Our base at Heston was before the war the home of the German Lufthansa Line flying civilian aircraft to Berlin. Hopefully one day we shall be flying far deadlier aircraft to Berlin with a mission very different from transporting tourists and business-men.

Our billets are in requisitioned council houses near by but most of our off duty time is spent in the Mess. It is wonderful to catch up with people like Squadron Leader Frey and Olek Gabsiewicz, to share so many memories and to hear so many different stories..

Now at last I feel I am flying again as I was trained to do. We are engaged mostly in Operation Rhubarb which means flying across the Channel and carrying out attacks at low level on roads, bridges, transport, electrical installations, railways and any other targets which might hamper the German war effort. My Grasshopper days certainly stand me in good stead now. The only drawback is the weather — the visibility is almost always bad which makes flying hazardous and difficult. The weather became worse and worse with thick fog and low cloud making flying almost impossible but the German Navy seized it as a golden opportunity to escape from Brest where the Gneisnau, the Scharnost and other ships had been holed up. They were very heavily defended and although numerous bombing attacks had been carried out the casualties were definitely more on our side than on theirs.

On 9th March two British pilots returning from one abortive mission radioed that they were on the move and difficult as it was their progress and whereabouts had to be monitored and plans for action made.

On 11th March they were reported in the Pas de Calais and a do-or-die operation to sink them began. This was led by a squadron of Swordfish from the Fleet Air Arm now based at Lee-on-Solent. They had been used with success at Taranto on the Italian coast and were equipped with torpedoes. They were led by Lieutenant Esmond, a man of conspicuous gallantry and determination.

We flew to Manston to refuel prior to acting as escort to the Swordfish. The weather was really atrocious. I remember that even seagulls and sparrows were strutting about on the ground, too wise to become air-borne, but we were under orders which did not apply to them. We were almost ready for take-off when the Swordfish emerged from the gloom but Lieutenant Esmond radioed that he could not wait even the odd minute for us, we must catch them up.

That was easier said than done as we flew towards Dunkirk, straining our eyes desperately to see ships, aircraft, anything moving under or around us. When we eventually located the battle area it was an absolute inferno. Every gun in the world seemed to be firing, aircraft were blazing, and Messerschmidts at low level were everywhere. Try as we might we could not penetrate the deadly curtain and eventually with fuel running low turned for home. Even then the danger was not over. In the nil visibility the tail wheel of my second pilot hit the top of my rudder and it was only by immense good fortune that we were both able to return safely to base.

The Swordfish, alas, did not share our good fortune. From the twelve which had set out so bravely only one survived. Sub-Lieutenant Lee managed to land on the Goodwin Sands with his air gunner killed and his observer wounded and was later picked up by sea. Some of the others, we have heard, were shot down into the sea and were rescued by the Germans and shut away in P.O.W. camps for the rest of the war. The others, including Lieutenant Esmond were killed.

On Friday 13th March I was again on escort duty with bombers going to Lille and for the first time had the opportunity to go into action against the Messerschmidts. Whether or not we had any success we did not know but at least I was fighting again and life was good.

17th APRIL 1942

The weather had relented at last. Fog and low cloud had given way to clear skies and it was a case of all systems go for us. Day after relentless day — sometimes twice a day — my fellow pilots and I attacked the Germans in one way or another. Sometimes we concentrated on Operation Rhubarb flying in at low level to strafe ground targets, sometimes we formed part of an escort for bombers. I could forget now the frustrations of former bomber escort duties when I had flown a Hurricane in close formation as the lowest tier of the protective umbrella, forbidden even to look for the enemy. Now in a Spitfire I reached the glorious heights where fighting was very much my business.

Once when escorting bombers to Ostend some German fighters dived on us. We made a rapid turn. One was actually firing at me from behind but he was not very accurate. In the mirror above my head I saw the smoking tracers of his fire. I turned very sharply and got him in my sights. I fired but was much too involved in the battle to wait and see what had happened to him. We had cameras on the wing of our aircraft which photographed the action automatically as soon as we opened fire and when these were developed on our return to base I was pleased to find that mine had turned out well and showed a Fokker Wolffe 190 damaged if not actually destroyed.

Today, 17th April — I had another golden opportunity and this time was really able to seize it. At about 35,000 feet over Boulogne we saw about twelve German aircraft chasing another squadron. We dived on them.

About 400 metres below me I saw a Fokker. He hadn't seen me. As soon as he came into my sights I 'pressed the tit' and my two canons and four machine guns opened up. The whole aircraft shook with the force of the fire and maybe I too was shaking with excitement and determination. This was for you, my Zosia, for my mother and family and friends and everyone enduring hunger and misery in Poland.

He turned slowly to the left. I corrected my aim. I knew that at any moment I might be fired on by his colleagues but the only thing that concerned me was that he must go down. Confound him! He seemed determined not to start smoking.

I fired a second and a third series into him, and this time he went into a spin and corkscrewed towards the ground. I had no chance to watch him any further. I had to join up with the rest of our aircraft for over France it was folly to be left alone.

There were aircraft higher up over the coast and for the moment I felt frightened and vulnerable. Were they ours or theirs? They were ours and thankfully I joined them to return to Heston. Now I had chance to look down and there, near the railway line to Boulogne, smoke and fire marked the funeral pyre of my victim. His aircraft had certainly gone and probably he had perished with it as I had seen no parachute opening.

I should perhaps have felt pity for him but there was no room in my heart for anything but a wild happiness. Altogether we had shot down five out of their twelve aircraft — and one of them was MINE! my first confirmed victory since I had come to England.

1st JULY 1942

Days merge into days with no realisation of time passing. My world has shrunk to the confines of my cockpit as we attack the whole coastline of northern France — Le Havre, Rouen, Boulogne, St Omer, Dunkirk, Lille — down to Ostend. Sometimes it is ground attacks, sometimes bombers to escort. There are Boston bombers now, beautiful but ferocious like huge mosquitoes with a deadly sting. So many German aircraft have been diverted to the Russian front that the Allies have a slight numerical advantage at last and we are making the most of it. There is work to be done — glorious long dreamed of work — and it absorbs my whole being.

I have been promoted to Flight-Lieutenant now and lead the squadron, to battle. It is a changed squadron. So many old comrades have gone, to higher positions, for weil-earned rest or to that special peace and rest from which they will never return. We have a lot of younger pilots, keen and well-trained, and they nickname me Daddy for I seem years older in age and experience. I need to be a real Daddy to them, someone to whom they can turn when things are hard, and I am doing what I can. I have more or less stopped drinking for I have no need of it any more.

What is happening in the world outside? We hear brief scraps of information but somehow it makes little impact. I am so tired that my brain outside flying has given up. Any fear that I once had of being shot down has vanished. I have seen it happen to too many and am resigned to it. It may happen in a fight, in an accident, or during one of those momentary episodes of blindness when the G-force of ultra-sharp turns and dives brings on a temporary blackout.

Often in the moments before I fall into sleep, pictures form in my mind. They are such vivid, unforgettable pictures. Oh for the pen of our great

Spitfire IX with Tadeusz and an adopted stray dog which became the mascot of the squadron at Heston. He was now a Flight-Lieutenant.

writers — Sienkiewicz, Zeromski — so that you could see them too, my Zosia, in all their beauty and their horror.

Flying high with the coasts of both France and England visible at the same time.

The uncaring sea below, the unmarked graveyard of so many. Greyish-white vapour trails like stripes against the blue sea. Little orange dinghies on the water. The white silk of parachutes drifting down,.

Strange spirals of aircraft, twisted like human lives. The sudden icing of the cockpit as I dive sharply from a height. An engine which seems to die then splutters defiantly to life.

These sights and sounds and so many like them will never leave me. They are part of the hunted and the hunting, of the terrifying tapestry of war in the sky.

10th JULY 1942

There were rumours that our tour of duty at Heston was coming to an end, but it was hard to believe. Everything seemed to be going as usual with the same ground sorties and escort duties, the same moments of satisfaction at duty well done outweighed by inevitable strain and frustration.

I was exhausted in body, mind and spirit which had an adverse effect on my tolerance level and made it difficult to recognise gradations between black and white, right and wrong.

Certainly my temper was on a very short fuse when returning to refuel after a hazardous Rhubarb sortie in which three of my pilots had been lost — one had gone down into the sea and I hoped was safe in his dinghy ready to be picked up, the other two unaccounted for — I saw a crowd of men and women workers sprawled on the concrete outside the two hangars used for the assembly and repair of much-needed aircraft. It was a warm, sunny day and they were plainly enjoying themselves, but why weren't they working?

"Oh, there's some sort of dispute because the sugar hasn't been delivered for their tea-break," the Intelligence Officer said when I asked him after the usual de-briefing.

He did not seem to be particularly interested or disturbed. After all, he was English and accustomed to taking petty disputes in his stride as part of working practices.

I was Polish, however, and did not even try to understand how workers could deliberately waste their war effort for a spoonful of sugar when service people were risking their lives, civilians starving and suffering, countries like Poland struggling in the relentless grip of the enemy and my own young pilots dead or missing.

White with rage, I said that when I took off again my hand might inexplicably slip on the controls and the fire-power of my Spitfire be directed at targets other than German aircraft or ground installations. He tried hard to take my words as a joke but his smile was a little sickly. I am sure it was not a coincidence that when we took off again there were no workers to be seen on the concrete, they were all safely inside whether back at work or not.

"Good for you, Daddy." came a soft, approving voice over the headphones from a pilot taking off with me. "The blighters thought you meant it."

"I'm not sure I didn't!" I said.

There was another occasion, far more serious, when the drastic action I felt should be taken was thwarted not by a last-minute touch of common-sense but by higher authority.

We were due to take-off at eight-thirty one morning on an important mission and I had put the squadron on readiness. Four of my young pilots had come to see me the day before and begged to be allowed to go up to London on a social engagement which obviously meant a lot to them. They swore that they would return early, sober, and ready to fly. Perhaps it was the memory of the days — centuries ago it now seemed — when I had been young with thought to spare for matters unconnected with war that made me give reluctant permission. I felt a shade uneasy at the time but this increased to anger and alarm when morning came and I found myself four pilots short.

There was no help for it. I had to rouse four sergeants who were on well-earned rest after a long stint of flying and ask them to fill the missing places. I was proud that they recognised the emergency and responded to a man but very worried lest in their tired, unprepared state they should come to harm. Thank God we all returned safely to base but I was in no mood to show leniency to the four culprits who had eventually turned up. There was no doubting their contrition as they explained that the car in which they were travelling had broken down but I was not prepared to accept any excuses. Dereliction of duty was a court martial offence and I was determined to see it through. They were spared only by the intervention of the Group Captain who recommended and gently but very firmly reinforced his decision that the consequences should be less severe than those I had demanded.

He explained that they had certainly learned their lesson once and for all and could be relied on never to offend again. They were young and foolish but excellent pilots whose potential must not be lost to the squadron. I like to believe that he was not influenced by the fact that two of them were connected with high-ranking officers of the Polish Air Force.

JULY 1942

It was true — we really were going off-readiness. For the moment we had done our share and it would be for other pilots to carry on the good work. Our feelings were very mixed, at least I know mine were. The hours of concentrated flying in the face of all that fate, the weather and the enemy could throw at us had taken their inevitable toll and sooner or later we would take risks which would cost not only our own lives but those of others. We badly needed a rest, a change, but what would we do. How would we survive life outside the cockpit of a Spitfire?

Meanwhile we had one last sortie to complete, a Rhubarb mission around Dieppe. It was obviously important as I was to lead twelve aircraft in sections of four with orders to destroy anything and everything we could find that was of importance to the enemy — electrical installations, gun emplacements, transport and so on. It would be up to us.

I think we were all slightly crazy as we took off, crossed the Channel, and cleared the greyish-white cliffs on the other side. This was our last chance to hit the Germans where it hurt and we were determined to make the most of it.

High-tension cables stretched before us with small brick transformer units. They presented a target which could only be reached at low level and I was determined to put my grasshopper training and experience to very good use. I tested my fire-power to make sure that all was well. The slow 'pak-pak' of the canons pounded like a pulse against the rattle of the machine-guns. My own heart pounded in unison as I turned and honed in, closely followed by the others. Flame sparked from the surface of the transformers and then smoke and fire spoke of success as we wheeled away.

Cows, grazing lazily in the meadows, turned and ran as we approached bellowing their fright at being chased by what must have seemed the biggest gadflies in the universe. Men working in the fields jumped from their tractors to lie flat in the furrows whilst one or two — good French Resistance sympathisers? — waved their caps in salute and encouragement.

I rounded a copse of trees and suddenly there was a German soldier with a gun mounted on a tripod. I was so low that I could see every detail of his fat red features and I knew that if he recovered from shock soon enough to fire I was doomed for he could not have missed me. I was flying parallel to him and could not turn in time to escape. I could only will him not to shoot as the rest of the squadron fired at the buildings and gun emplacements to which he belonged. For the moment I thought he had hit me as there was a strange whipping noise on my fuselage but my instruments were all right and my engine functioning as normal and I realised that I had actually hit some of the high tension cable and taken it with me.

We came upon a small chateau with cars and lorries parked in the grounds and a couple of people on the terrace. One or two of them were soldiers in uniform but there were a number of civilians including women and children. They gasped at us and tried to scatter whilst one German officer drew his revolver and aimed at me in desperation. Were they one of our targets? Even as the thought flashed across my mind I knew that I could not deliberately kill women and children and gave the order not to fire.

The roads seemed empty of any transport and there was nothing moving on the railways. Close by the railway was a works with a tall chimney and a number of metal tanks. A distillery, perhaps? We set it on fire for good measure and headed for the coast and our return journey to England. We had flown in so low that the coastal guns had no chance to open fire on us, but they were ready for our return.

We had to fly through quite a heavy barrage and one of my pilots called he had been hit. I asked him to test his instruments and engines but thankfully they were all right and he was able to take his place with us. Halfway across the Channel we were warned by radio that there were Messerschmidts chasing us and my neck nearly became detached from my shoulders as I scanned the sky in all directions.

Luckily we saw nothing and landed safely at Heston, all twelve of us. Some of the aircraft had suffered damage of a fairly harmless kind and the high tension cable had left its mark on mine to the consternation of my ground crew. It was over! Nothing remarkable had been achieved but we had done what we had been asked to do and the details remain in my mind simply because it was the end.

A few days later we were told that General Sikorski had flown in on a brief visit to see us and to present decorations. A number of both flying personnel and ground crew had been awarded the Polish Air Force Medal which, in contrast to British decorations, is awarded to all ranks alike who have distinguished themselves in the performance of their duties. These medals had not yet been struck so could not be actually handed over until later.

Wacek Krol was awarded the Virtuti Militari which is the highest battle decoration of all the Polish services. Various other pilots including myself were awarded the Cross of Valour. It was good to be recognised for those achievements which now belonged to the past although it was the future which now occupied our minds.

At the end of July we flew out from Heston to Hutton Cranswick, a small airfield on the edge of the Yorkshire Wolds, where we were to rest and wait for our various postings. It was a wry stroke of fate that led to one of our pilots colliding with a straw stack and killing himself, a tragic accident which perhaps illustrated how close we all were to the end of our reserves.

I was bewildered and by no means delighted to find that I had been posted to Montrose in Scotland to the Instructors Flying Training School. An entirely new phase of my flying life was certainly about to start.

22nd NOVEMBER 1942

My journey to Montrose lasted for a whole day and night although to me it seemed that it would never end. I do not know how efficient British railways were before the war but certainly under present conditions travelling was an endurance test. Whatever my warrant might have entitled me to as an officer there was no question of a seat in a first-class carriage — it was a case of finding space available in corridors already crowded beyond capacity, and that was when I was actually on a train! The journey involved constant changes and long waits at various stations.

I remember the misery of a long wait at a station which I think was Grantham. I was cold, thirsty, hungry and generally fed-up. I saw a hut which I was told housed a canteen run by the Salvation Army which is a religious organisation devoted to helping those in need. More in desperation than in hope I pushed open the door and envied the people that I saw drinking hot tea and eating buns and sandwiches. There was a cheerful looking woman behind a trestle counter dressed in a navy dress with a navy beribboned bonnet on her head and I managed to push my way through to her.

"Please," I said, "I am a Roman Catholic but I would give anything for a hot cup of tea!"

I shall always remember her kindly laughter.

"My dear boy, it doesn't matter if you are the Devil himself," she said, "if you want a cup of tea you shall have one."

Bless her heart. I shall always be grateful to her as a real Christian who saved my reason if not my life.

Eventually I was on a train crossing the wonderful Forth Bridge and had time to marvel at such a feat of engineering which I had seen in pictures before the war. Then at last — at long last — I arrived at Montrose and was driven three or four miles to the Air Force Instructors Flying Training School. The Mess was in a really beautiful country house and I was taken to my room in one of the wooden barracks nearby where at last I was able to wash and shave and transform myself into a semblance of an officer.

Lunch in the Mess cheered me further but my spirits finally rose when I had an interview with the Wing Commander. He was kind and welcoming and seemed to understand exactly how I felt at being, as I saw it, kicked into a dead-end job. He had my records from 316 and showed a great deal of interest in all we had done. He explained that most of the officers had been on operations and that our skill and experience were badly needed in the training of others. I would learn just how this could be done quickly and efficiently but meanwhile I was to look upon the course as well-merited recreation and enjoy it.

I was pleased to find that I had two fellow Poles — Flying Officer Czarnecki and Pilot Officer Wieck — amongst my colleagues who had arrived slightly before me. Czarnecki and I became friends although I had not met him previously and it was good to speak Polish and exchange experiences.

The surrounding countryside was really beautiful with forests of all kinds and we formed the habit of going for long walks when not needed for lectures and flying. On an early walk Czarnecki suddenly let out a yell of pleasure — he had spotted mushrooms under the trees which were exactly like those of home. We picked as many as we could and returned in triumph to the Mess where we begged an onion and some margarine before going to my room. There was a metal wash-basin on a stand and a two-bar electric stove and we had soon washed the mushrooms, sliced them, and put them in the basin to cook.

The smell! It brought back so many memories besides attracting the interest and curiosity of English colleagues who came to see what was happening. They were horrified to find us eating what they called toadstools and were sure we would die of poisoning although one or two of them dared to have a taste and admitted it was delicious. The next day people looked to see if we were still alive and healthy and finding that we were asked us to get more mushrooms and invite them to the feast. Eventually the Group-Captain himself joined in and gave us a day off to collect as many mushrooms as we could which we cooked in proper pans in the kitchen this time. The senior officers' wives were invited to come along and after some hesitation tasted, feasted and were more than ready to learn how to collect and cook mushrooms for themselves.

We certainly made our mark from that angle but Czarnecki was to distinguish himself in a more dramatic way. On one of his low-flying exercises over the mountains and high moorland he spotted what looked like an aircraft. He circled and flew even lower for a closer inspection and that convinced him that he was right. Its canvas superstructure was so camouflaged by the bracken surrounding it that it would have been invisible from a normal height and the site was remote from any roads or habitation. His report was received with a certain amount of cynicism but an expedition was mounted and there, just as it had been for some twenty-five years, was a single seater Camel from the First World War which had crashed with its undercarriage torn away but was otherwise intact. The pilot was still in the cockpit. Poor devil! No one had known his fate or his whereabouts and his family must have been tormented as were so many others by the chilling tag 'missing'. Now he could be identified and given back to them for Christian burial and it was all owing to the sharp eyes of another pilot in another war who had been forced out of his own country so far away and eventually found himself in Scotland. God certainly works in mysterious ways.

As the only Poles on the course we soon found ourselves forgetting national differences and being accepted as comrades and friends. I began for the first time to understand the British and the British way of life and to discover how few were the differences and how many the similarities between us. We had the same love of our country, the same determination to defeat the Germans, but whilst we tended to talk about it they hid their deepest feelings behind what seemed at first to be a flippant couldn't-care-less attitude. They found release in schoolboy pranks and jokes and the cultivation of whatever social life was available.

I remember a group of us descending on the village hall of a remote place lost in the forests where a dance was taking place. Most of the guests were Land Army girls from the Forestry Commission in their thick breeches and green jerseys who did not allow the absence of men to interfere with their enjoyment of a rare break in routine. Not that that deterred them from showing exuberant delight at the sight of us.

"Men!" they cried with as much excitement as if we had been from another planet and they made quite sure that we enjoyed the evening as much as they evidently did.

On another occasion we were invited to a dance at a hospital some miles away and piled into our transport with hopes of another warm welcome. We were not disappointed and I managed to forget that it was no ordinary hospital but a mental institution even though I had always been terrified of such places. It was only when I was walking through the trees back to our waiting transport with the delightful nurse who was my partner for the evening that alarm struck. I could hear the sound of an axe splitting logs which seemed a strange sound in the darkness.

"Oh that's only Bill!" my companion said airily. "He's only happy when he's using his axe!"

I had visions of some demented giant coming at me from behind every tree and was amazed at the calm acceptance of this young girl. I was certainly glad to be on my way back to Montrose!

As we had been told, our stay at Montrose offered us rest and recreation but there was serious side to it as well. Our lecturers went out of their way to make things clear and interesting and for all our limited grasp of English we were able to follow what we were told. Long ago — before the war — I had trained pilots on the airfield at Warsaw. Now a lot of useful knowledge had been grafted onto that experience and by the time I received my Instructors' Diploma I had a far greater awareness of what was involved and how to pass on my skills as a pilot.

I had resented being sent to Montrose but I had gained a lot, felt rested and refreshed, and even knew regret when it was time to leave.

Where now, I wondered? Back to the squadron as I was secretly hoping? No! My course at Montrose had been for a definite purpose. My posting was as an instructor to the Polish Flying School at Newton in Nottinghamshire.

22nd NOVEMBER 1943

I have not written in my diary for a year now — there has been nothing to write. I am sunk once more in a deep trough of despair and hopelessness and can see no way out of it. The situation in Poland is growing worse and worse and I have had almost no news of my family or of you, my Zosia. What is happening? What will happen? What can I do to end this terrible war when I am held in limbo? When I was with the squadron I could fight knowing that if I were to die it would be in a good cause. At Montrose I learned skills to offer in passing on knowledge and experience to younger pilots who were so badly needed as Allied losses mounted. Now — nothing!

The Polish Flying Training School at Newton is entirely Polish right down to the W.A.A.F. personnel. You would imagine that I would feel at home here surrounded by my own people but I feel completely isolated. The instructors and senior officers are older than I am, the pupils almost young enough to be my sons.

A few — a very few — of the senior officers have fought in the Battle of Britain where they showed great gallantry and deserved the decorations they wear with so much pride but they now feel they have earned a quiet life and are making the most of it. The ones who have seen no action have no ambition to do so and seem quite fulfilled by the day-to-day routine of slowly developing the flying skills of their pupils to no apparent purpose. Their programme is laid down by R.A.F. Cranwell who, as far as I can see, have no real confidence in the vital part that the Poles might give to the war effort and show little enthusiasm other than for keeping them quiet and contented and out of the way.

It would not be true to say that my colleagues have no idea that there is a war on for they talk about it endlessly to each other and to the English people they meet on social occasions. They bemoan the fate of our country and blame everything and everyone that has contributed to it but seem resigned to being victims of misfortune rather than showing any zeal to put matters right by their own efforts. I suppose I find it specially hard after Montrose where I learned to work hard, play hard, and hide emotion behind jokes and laughter with the determination never to give in.

The youngsters who are our pupils vary considerably in their reactions and I can quite understand how they feel. I compare their training with mine so long ago. War was far from our thoughts but we knew our flying skills were being developed not as an end in themselves but as a means of defending our country by those skills should the need arise. Now these young men are simply undergoing an extension of their initial flying training, getting in more flying hours, and for what? Now in the midst of the toughest war in history they are in the position of someone learning to control a car really well without realising that he will be expected to take to the high-road and face the hazards and challenges involved. They may have been keen once but now they seem resigned to an everlasting routine of circuits and landings and occasional cross-country flights. We do not even fly from Newton where there are no proper runways but from Tollerton, a small airfield just outside Nottingham, where the facilities are limited indeed.

They not only lack purpose, they lack the iron discipline imposed on us which is essential in the development of that inner discipline which turns a pilot into a fighter. I think back to the hardships we endured — the seemingly impossible tasks, the unquestioning obedience of orders, the lack of any excuses for the slightest deviation from the standard required. Perhaps it was too harsh but at least we knew that we could accomplish anything asked of us and it brought us through the nightmare we endured.

Some of them are docile enough, quite content to do what is asked of them and save their real energy for their social lives and the numerous local girls who flock around them like bees round a honey-pot. Others — and I can see my younger self numbered amongst them — are bored and rebellious and vent their feelings by unorthodox flying whenever they can escape from their instructors. They try out manoeuvres and aerobatics which they have not been trained to do safely, often with tragic results. Soon after my arrival two were killed trying out aerobatics at far too low a level in order to impress their girl friends. I had to identify them and was sickened and shaken by the waste of young lives — it was so much worse than those I had known who had been killed in action.

Another youngster was killed needlessly on a cross-country flight when the weather clamped down and he lost his bearings. I was in touch with him by radio — can you imagine how I felt? He was in such a state of panic that advice and instructions were lost on him and he might as well not have had a compass for all the use he made of it. Ultimately there was silence as he ran out of fuel and plunged into the North Sea.

Accidents, accidents! And so many of them preventable.

I have become highly unpopular all round trying to shake some sense into the system. I take to the air myself whenever I can as a 'spy in the sky' looking for pupils flying in a way they should not do in places where they should not be and coming down as hard as I can on the culprits. I make what they see as unreasonable demands on them although one or two

A pastel cartoon drawn by one of the pupils at Tollerton. It describes Tadeusz as the 'Ragamuffin Tyrant'.

two have shown signs of responding. If only I had the equipment, the facilities to offer them.

I have managed to gain the co-operation of at least two of my fellow instructors who despite never having seen action have excellent flying skills and far more patience with the young than I have. I try to influence their attitude to training and arouse their interest in putting into effect as sound a programme as the circumstances make possible whilst they in turn try to turn me into a better representation of the 'officer and gentleman' they feel lurks below my surface.

I'll admit that it's a long way below the surface. As always when I am frustrated and fed up I am morose and bad-tempered and seek to drown my feelings in drink. It's no wonder that the majority of my colleagues have given me up for lost when I make no effort to be anything but awkward.

The Group Captain and senior officers do their best to provide as good a social life as possible with dances, dinners, and concerts to which local people are invited so that we fit into the community and do not feel isolated and alien. Invitations abound into people's homes for the plight of us Poles seems to have captured the sympathy and imagination of the English and they are warm in their wish to show their concern.

I obstinately refuse to have any part in it. Whenever possible, especially on Wednesdays which is our official half-day, I escape into Nottingham and find my own entertainment particularly at the Palais de Danse in the company of one or two like-minded cronies. Here there are girls to talk to and dance with quite without commitment, bright lights, music — in short escapism.

Here too for a month or so I found solace and enjoyment of a better kind in the company of a bomber crew based at R.A.F. Bottesford. They were a great set of lads full of the spirit I had known in the squadron. The pilot was American and the others were an assortment of Australians, New Zealanders and Canadians. With them I felt really in tune and could forget everything in the jokes we shared, the lively conversations.

We decided that the price of drinks in the bar was too high for our limited resources and took bottles of whatever we could find, bribing a waitress to bring us a very large teapot with the harmless-looking afternoon tea we ordered. Into this we tipped whatever we had which was a potent brew indeed and it is not surprising that people around were amazed at how merry we got on a cup of tea.

I shall never forget the day when one of the group turned up alone. The crew had flown on a mission the night before and he had stayed behind as reserve having a head cold. Like so many others they did not return and their fate was as yet unknown. It must have cost him a great deal to come and bring me the news in person. I knew how he felt having lost so many good friends both in Poland and since but it must have been even more devastating for him as one of a crew who had shared everything together.

That was war — that is war — and I have no useful part to play in bringing it to a satisfactory end. That is a particular hell which I have lived through before and find now even more difficult. Is it any wonder that I feel I am going crazy?

10th MARCH 1944

At the end of November my black mood which caused me to behave in such an uncooperative way very nearly cost me my career and any hopes I might have had of returning to active life as a fighter-pilot.

I was circling the airfield at Tollerton after one of my 'spying missions' checking on my pupils when I saw a group of people who were obviously very senior officers judging by the scrambled egg on their hats and fat rings on their sleeves. It seemed to me to be the last straw. Here was I held against my will in a job which gave me no satisfaction and only drove me to desperation and there were they puffed up with their own importance caring nothing for the damage their dictates gave not only to me but to the young pilots in my charge.

Furious resentment gave way to a temporary madness as I, determined to teach them a lesson they could not ignore, dived in so low over their heads that they had literally to fling themselves on the ground and flew off again laughing like a maniac.

It was no surprise when I eventually landed to be greeted by two Red Caps who ordered me politely but very firmly to report immediately to the main officer where Air Vice-Marshall Cunningham wanted to speak to me.

I had not realised quite how high and mighty were my victims but I do not think it would have altered my conduct if I had. I knew I had asked for trouble of a very serious kind and was ready to face the music.

The Air Vice-Marshall, accompanied by the Wing Commander Flying from Cranwell, left me in no possible doubt as to their opinion of my crime. I listened stony-faced to what was said and had to admit that it was more than justified. I steeled myself for the inevitable.

When it came, it took me completely by surprise. The Air Vice-Marshall looked closely at me, and although his expression was still one of icy disapproval, there was just a hint of humour in his eyes. "You don't like being here at Newton, do you?" he barked. "Why?"

I took a deep breath and fought hard to master my command of the English language. He had asked me a straight question and something told me that he was prepared to listen whilst I answered it. And listen he did with an attention that I knew I had not merited as I poured out all my frustrations; not as far as I personally was concerned but the difficulties

I met on every hand in being able to give my pupils the training in active combat they needed to became valuable pilots.

His questions were shrewd and penetrating, my answers frank and factual. For the moment rank was almost forgotten, we were two people completely committed to supplying the Allied Forces with the right number of pilots of the right calibre. "What equipment do you need to do the job properly?" he asked.

I had my shopping list all ready — had I not pleaded for these vital items over and over only to be put off with the stories of shortages? Now I voiced them all: cine cameras for the wings of the aircraft, films, projectors, screens and the rest of it. The Wing-Commander looked on aghast. He had clearly expected the floor to be wiped once and for all with this insignificant Pole whose constant requests had irked him. Now the Air Vice-Marshall appeared to be taking him seriously.

He was even more aghast the next moment when the Air Vice-Marshall thumped the table in front of him.

"See that he gets everything!" he ordered. "Tomorrow!" He brushed aside complaints that it would all take time to produce so much so soon.

"I shall telephone him personally next week to make sure he has all that he needs," he said.

Incredibly, everything arrived and I was able to assure the Air Vice-Marshall when he telephoned as promised that the new training regime was already underway.

"Splendid," he said. "Draw up your programme and let me have a copy straight away. I shall come in three weeks to see the progress you have made. If I am satisfied I promise you will soon return to the squadron. If not you will be here for the rest of your flying life."

It was a tough challenge but one I was determined to meet. There were no more stupid escapades, no evenings wasted in drunken stupor. There were only four of us as instructors on Harvards and I was lucky to gain their co-operation. One in particular, Zygmunt Zakrzewski, became my right-hand man and close friend. None of them had had combat experience but all were very skilled pilots and excelient instructors. Once they knew what we were aiming at they could pass it on to our pupils with far more patience than I had.

The whole attitude of the pupils changed miraculously too. There were few problems of discipline or slackness as they realised for the first time what they were meant to be doing and given a definite purpose for the future. They listened attentively to lessons on tactics and manoeuvres knowing that they would soon put them into practice. They were thrilled by actual fighting exercises when cameras on the aircraft wings recorded exactly what and when they had accomplished. These films were analysed in frank detail and their ambition was ignited.

We managed to acquire the use of a small range in a clearing of the woods beside the Fosse and were able to practise dive-bombing with smoke bombs at targets painted on the ground. I hoped that no one knew I was only one step ahead of those I trained! My fighting experience had been confined to canons and machine guns and I had to study my manuals far into the night in order to pass on the right instructions.

When Air Vice-Marshall made his promised visit he expressed himself delighted with what a gimlet-eyed inspection revealed whilst at the same time offering useful hints for still greater achievement.

I still longed to return to active service and was buoyed up by the belief that the Air Vice-Marshall would keep his side of the bargain and use his influence on my behalf. However life had a purpose again and I was no longer a complete pain to myself and to all those unfortunate enough to be with me.

My social life improved, too. When the Poles had taken over at Newton, the English Group-Captain had approached various local people with the suggestion that they might be willing to entertain some of these officers so far from home. Sir Alick Birkin and his wife Louie were amongst those who had volunteered and for some time a group of officers including Zygmunt Zakrzewski and Edouard Susinski had enjoyed having dinner, listening to music, playing games, dancing and generally enjoying the warmth and welcome offered by their host and hostess and the friends they had invited to join in. Like the black sheep of the family, I had been excluded from such festivities and to be honest even if I had been invited I would have rejected such an offer.

Now, however, I was doing my best to shake off my wild image and the Palais de Danse had lost all its appeal since the loss of my friends, the Lancaster crew. I was ready if not enthusiastic for Edouard and Zygmunt to ask if I might receive an invitation to the next social evening.

By now Sir Alick, who was considerably older than his wife, had died but Louie found comfort in the companionship of the Poles she had got to know, particularly that of Edouard. He was a very kind, gentle man who knew what it was to be lonely for he had left his wife and two sons behind in Poland. Zygmunt too had a wife and son in Poland so that she could enjoy their support without any threat of emotional commitment. They were both at pains to impress upon me the need to behave like a gentleman. My mind instinctively went back over the years to the encounter my friends and I had had with a Polish lady in Paris. "They are not Polish gentlemen, they are swine!" she had told her little daughter. Now I must try to avoid gaining a similar reputation here in England.

As I had anticipated, the party atmosphere was a little too quiet and formal to appeal. However, the food was good, the welcome warm, and there was plenty to drink. My colleagues and Louie's friends behaved admirably and I blotted my copy book only once when I volunteered to demonstrate my ability to drink a glass of whisky upside down whilst propped against a wall. It was received with polite laughter but one of the girls was like Victoria, definitely not amused.

Louie was about to leave her big manor house for a smaller modern house in the same village but the social evenings continued on a less formal scale with buffets replacing the dinners. I became friendly with some of the girls and received invitations to play tennis with two of them which I enjoyed.

I even played my part when we entertained them at Mess dances when they appeared very glamorous in full evening dress although with petrol practically non-existent for civilians they had cycled to Newton with their dresses in carrier bags hung from the handlebars. One lady was a farmer's wife who supplied pigs to the Mess for which she was allowed petrol. She hit on the idea of delivering a young pig on the same evening as a dance and piled everyone into the car with it. Unfortunately the pig escaped during the evening causing havoc as well as amusement on the dance floor. I began to appreciate the ingenuity and initiative of the English women, their refusal to allow Hitler to destroy their lives more than was absolutely necessary.

They began to relax towards me, too, and find my antics amusing compared with the old-fashioned gallantry displayed by the others. I enjoyed their friendship and was looking for nothing else for I was still engaged to Zosia and planning to return and marry her when the war was won. I had not heard from her or of her for many months as correspondence with Poland was limited indeed so I did not know if she had found someone else or indeed if she were still alive. I had my perfect alibi however if any girl sensed a romantic commitment.

I needed no alibi as far as Diana was concerned. She it was who had not been amused by my whisky-on-my-head demonstration at our first meeting and she continued to make it plain that her opinion had not changed. It irked my pride even if I found her reserve and seeming inability to let her hair down by no means attractive.

And then at last it happened! Air Vice-Marshall Cunningham had kept his side of our bargain and on 14th March I received orders to join the squadron at R.A.F. Speke near Liverpool. I was wild with relief and excitement and in the mood to enjoy to the full the farewell evening Louie gave for me as she had for one or two others who had been posted from Newton.

I was determined to crown the evening and get Diana to notice me and, abetted by my colleagues who were aware of and amused by the situation, managed to get her on her own for a moment and pin a Polish eagle on her dress.

"Please write to me when I am back in the Squadron," I pleaded.

She was clearly hesitant but she was already writing to some of the others to show that someone cared when they were in danger and conscience forbade her to refuse.

"You can help to correct my English," I said, "and I will correct your Polish."

The bargain was sealed with a chaste kiss on the cheek. Now I could depart in triumph with my great ambition to get the training programme established fulfilled and this much less significant ambition fulfilled too. It was a good omen.

Squadron, I thought, here I come. Here where my heart lies, where there is real work to be done . . .

27th APRIL, 1944

It was wonderful to be back with the Squadron although as so often seemed to happen my hopes were not completely fulfilled. The sixteen months I had spent away from active service, first at Montrose then at Newton, had brought inevitable changes. Those of my colleagues who had returned to operations after a few months' rest had learned new techniques, new skills, new ways to handle aircraft which had developed amazingly from the ones I had flown. They were obviously superior to me and I sensed they were aware of this, however friendly they might be. Besides that there were a number of far younger pilots whom I did not know and who looked upon me as an old has-been which at thirty-one years old was a bit hard to take.

However, I enjoyed a couple of days familiarising myself with the Spitfire Mark Nine and then my Squadron-Leader and friend Wacek Krol sent me up to Peterhead which was the Central Bombing Training School. Dive bombing was becoming increasingly part of the Squadron's job and my knowledge of it was limited to the study of manuals I had undertaken in order to instruct my pupils at Newton. I threw myself into my task with determination and did not find it too difficult, progressing quickly to the bombing of live targets in the sea where a direct hit sent satisfactory fountains of salt water into the air.

Exactly a week later, on 27th March, I returned to Speke where I was just in time to join in the whirl of activity caused by the news that a new phase of operations was imminent. As part of the Second Tactical Air Force we were moving South to a series of temporary air fields. We were issued with folding canvas beds, canvas wash-basins, tents and the like which were loaded onto a lorry together with the few personal possessions and one suitcase each which was the limit we were allowed.

Some of my younger colleagues greeted the prospect with disquiet. Their days till now had been spent in the civilised comfort of established aerodromes with well-furnished rooms, hot water on tap, and meals cooked and served in some style. It was my turn now to feel superior! I looked forward to the new conditions which brought vivid memories of scouting camps and my initial training. I knew I should quickly find ways to make myself reasonably comfortable even though as luck would have it the weather was bitingly cold. Maybe now I would not go as far as to bury myself in a convenient manure heap in order to keep warm!

The airfield near Lewes bore out many people's worst forebodings when we flew in. It was quite literally a field with a runway formed from a strip of reinforced wire netting pegged to the ground to keep it flat. There were no creature comforts of any kind but true to my resolve I set about remedying any deficiencies for myself. A sack stuffed with straw and dead leaves made a useful palliasse placed on top of the low canvas bed and the idea quickly caught on.

Washing was a problem with water rationed to a share from the tank brought to the site each day for cooking, drinking, washing and all other purposes. Remembering my scouting days I found a tin in which I punched holes, a forked branch which I fixed firmly in the ground, and an extra fuel tank which I 'liberated' from the stock standing ready to be fixed onto our aircraft when needed. I also borrowed one of the stirrup pumps which were in good supply. I collected wood for a fire, heated water in the tank and used the stirrup pump to fill the holed tin which then made an excellent shower. It was a far better solution than that favoured by the others which was to cycle to the nearest hotel and beg for a bath for which they were charged £1 much to their dismay. Wacek Krol saw my invention and begged to share it whilst asking me not to pass on the method to the others or water would be scarce. I even built a fireplace of turfs outside the open flaps of my tent and lit a wood fire with the smoke escaping through a chimney of tins joined by clay and was able to sleep warm and snug.

As to food cooked in the portable camp kitchen when it was cooked at all (it was more often than not corned beef) that was a real hardship but I could not afford to supplement my diet with meals in local restaurants. In free time I visited local farms by cycle hoping to buy eggs but was told that they were severely rationed. The egg-packing station collected them each week and issued food for the hens in return depending strictly on the number collected. The civilian population would eventually receive one egg every week. However — and this was my salvation — goose eggs were not rationed and I was able to get a supply and take them back to the airfield where I scrambled them in a tin with some begged margarine from the cookhouse. Like the mushrooms in Montrose, this was a meal to be shared and enjoyed with Wacek and other friends.

We lived the life of gypsies, moving from one improvised airfield to another in South-eastern England as need dictated. Conditions were always the same but others were learning to adapt to them as I did and it was gratifying to be consulted as a wise old man instead of a dotard!

Our work-load in the air was heavy but I know none of us resented it. It was all to an excellent purpose for although no one breathed so much as a word of it I think we all knew that the longed for invasion was on the cards at last and that we were helping to pave the way for it.

For the first time in the war we had air superiority and there was hardly a German aircraft to be seen. Day and night we escorted wave after wave of bombers across the Channel to drop their lethal cargo on industrial areas and we flew our own missions too over the Channel coast. This time we had not only our canons and machine-guns to destroy our targets but the bombs we had trained to use, screaming down from the skies in dives from 5,000 feet to barely 200 feet which must have been terrifying to those below. The only opposition we encountered as we attacked military installations, roads, bridges and transport of all kinds was from anti-aircraft guns massed in great numbers. Our briefings took us mainly away from the actual coastline and in particular from Normandy.

It was tiring work needing absolute concentration but even the fact that I no longer led the Wing but was under the direction of pilots often younger than I was did not spoil my satisfaction in what I was doing.

We were all caught up in the excitement and wanted our part in it. This — tragically — went as high as my dear Colonel Pawlikowski who had been my idol, my saviour in trouble right from the early days in Poland. Unable to restrain his longing to be in action rather than commanding his men from the ground, he insisted on replacing a pilot on one of our missions and was brought down by enemy gunfire, one of our amazingly few casualties.

No one ever learned exactly how he had died but I prayed it would have been a quick death without time for fear or suffering. He deserved that if anyone ever did.

I shall never forget him.

15th MAY 1944

It is a miracle that I am able to add this entry to my diary. 7th May may so easily — so very easily — have seen the end not only of my career as a pilot but of my life itself. It started so very happily. Squadron-Leader Krol sent me to try out the brand-new aircraft which had been allocated to me. It had flown for only 12 hours and was in absolutely peak condition.

I walked slowly round it, taking in every detail. It had my own sign on the fuselage WX-E. I patted it lovingly. "Lovely one," I said, "I will make good use of you."

The ground crew stood around watching me, smiling at my happiness and assuring me that everything was O.K. I climbed into the cockpit, started the engine, and taxied to the starting point on the runway. Another pilot took off and now it was my turn.

I opened the engine slowly and began to taxi. More throttle. The arrow on the speedometer moved to 60 mils–70 mils The airflow began to get under the wings and I tried to get airborne but still had not enough speed. I could hear the dull thudding of the shock absorbers on the rough runway. 75–80 mils Now!

Suddenly I heard a loud crack and the aircraft jerked to the left. The airstreams under the wings were still too weak to lift me.

I realised a tyre had burst. I opened the throttle fully and tugged frantically on the joy-stick. I might be lucky. No good. I turned off the switches and applied the opposite brake. The end of the runway was in sight. I could see the beginning of soft ground ahead.

The second tyre burst.

The tail began to lift.

Instinctively I covered my face with one arm before losing consciousness.

It was dark. My head ached. I could not move. I realised I was trapped in the aircraft which was now upside down, pressing me into the ground with its weight. God! Three tons of metal and petrol and I was powerless to move.

I tried desperately to release myself somehow. I felt that I was suffocating. Worst of all in the stillness I could hear the hiss of petrol dripping from the additional tank onto the red-hot exhaust pipes. God save me! Don't let me be burned alive.

I twisted and pulled on my hands, trying to release them but my right arm was under the opening of the fuselage. I managed somehow to release my safety belt but it didn't help.

My head was in such a position that my chin was clamped to my chest. Air! Air!

I was growing weaker and becoming resigned. I was begging quietly: "Do help me! Somebody help me!" But there was no one. My eyes, buried in sand, could see nothing but a redness. The fire had started. It was the end. I realised that the redness was not fire but the light of the indicator and made the effort to free myself yet again but I couldn't move.

I said goodbye to everyone I love — my mother, Zosia, my family — and asked God to help me.

There was a tug on my hand. Magically help had arrived. Dimly I realised that I could move my head a little and so get a little air. There was a noise. Somebody was dragging me from under the aircraft. My eyes were burning agonisingly but I was aware of a little daylight. Now I was being lifted and carried. Happiness flooded over me and I thanked God as I drifted into unconsciousness.

I came to to find myself surrounded by doctors and nurses. I was in the

Field Hospital. Everyone was asking me if I felt sick and went on asking me. I found later that the metal plate at the back of the aircraft seat had bent over my head and they were frightened I had a skull fracture. All that concerned me, though, was my eyes. I begged for them to be bathed so that the sand could be washed out and I would be able to see.

The medical staff were incredulous when in a day or so I was almost recovered apart from having two beautiful black eyes and eyeballs suffused with blood. Despite the urgency of the times I was sent on leave to recuperate and returned to Newton where Zygmunt and my other friends did their best to get my spirits back.

It was not easy because there had been news that Edouard Susinski was missing, believed killed. He had been posted soon after I left and was flying bombing missions on Mosquitoes. He and Zygmunt had been close friends as had he and Louie. She was devastated by the news and whenever he was not on duty Zygmunt cycled over to be with her and try to cheer her. Naturally under the circumstances there were no social gatherings at her house.

I decided to cycle over to see Diana whose letters I had enjoyed and whom I now looked upon as a friend even if there was nothing more between us. She was startled to see me as I had given her no warning but my battered features aroused her sympathy and I was invited in to have tea with the Aunt and Uncle with whom she lived and the rest of the family.

I felt at home with them straight away, particularly with her Aunt who reminded me so much of my beloved mother, and I behaved very correctly as I was served with tea on a lace tablecloth with a silver tea service, fine china cups, and delicate cucumber sandwiches with the crusts removed. I basked in their sympathy and was delighted by their invitation to return as often as I liked

Diana still kept her distance and I gathered her interests lay elsewhere but I did not really mind. It was enough to have somewhere warm and welcoming to go even if at my subsequent visits formality was abandoned and I had the usual wartime tea in the kitchen with the rest of the family.

Everyone knew that the invasion was imminent and that my days at Newton were few. I told Diana that when I said in my letters that I was tired and fed up, she would know that I was back in action.

5th JUNE 1944

I returned to the Squadron on 21st May, the Medical Officer at Newton having passed me fit for flying. I really think I would have committed murder or suicide if he hadn't. I just couldn't have borne to be shunted onto the sidelines again when I knew that the most momentous phase of

Members of 302 Squadron, the 'Swallows', relax 'Somewhere in England' before the invasion of Europe in June 1944.

the war was about to start. I had to be there, playing my part, no matter what the future might have in store for me.

The sense of urgency was more than confirmed when I rejoined my colleagues. There was work to be done and no one gave a thought to anything else. We flew continual sorties over the Channel, this time concentrating on dive-bombing roads, bridges, military installations and supply columns not on the coast but inland so that the German forces could not bring up reinforcements except during the hours of darkness. We escorted wave after wave of heavy bombers as they dropped their deadly loads. We patrolled the English south coast looking for bandits. We had almost complete air superiority and I rejoiced in it with all my heart. Now we were giving back all that we had been forced to take in Poland, in Britain, in so many parts of Europe devastated by Hitler and his colleagues.

The only concession forced on me by Wacek Krol was that I must have longer rest periods between sorties even though I did my best to convince him that my battered rainbow-hued features did not indicate my inability to fly.

There was no room for argument in the present climate and I had the sense to realise it. Our lives were now completely disciplined and there was no time for individual needs and preferences.

We moved constantly from one airfield to another and once on the ground were not allowed to move outside. All the letters we sent or received were censored and we could make no telephone calls. Drinking was absolutely forbidden, everything being put in bond. I was on the verge of serious trouble when I was found with a few colleagues finding consolation in downing copious quantities of cider but no one had dreamed of its alcoholic content until its effects were made clear so it had escaped the ban. It was a situation soon remedied.

I knew that everything was ready for the coming onslaught but even so could not have dreamed in advance of the intensity of the preparations. Every road within miles of the South Coast was packed solid with tanks, armoured vehicles, and guns. Every open space was a rash of tents. Every smallest creek and inlet on the coast was crammed with ships of all kinds. Only the weather threatened delay and no one had any control over that.

On June 3rd we moved to the airfield near Chichester which was just a flat field with no runway so that so could only pray that the ground would not hamper taking-off and landing. We were summoned to a house not far from the air field where we found the Group-Captains of the 2nd Tactical Air Force including our own Olek Gabrzewski.

Here our situation as Poles was spelled out to us gravely and clearly. We could expect no mercy if we were shot down over enemy territory for Poland had long since fallen under German rule and we would be treated as escapees at best or traitors at worst. We were to carry revolvers at all times. We were issued with maps printed on fine silk squares which could be folded and hidden unobtrusively on our bodies and with money in the necessary currencies.

We even acquired British identities and were given new identity bracelets. My name was now John Barlow and I was to stick to it through thick and thin. If shot down we were to escape through Spain or by any means possible, Spain and Portugal having given secret agreement to help us get back to England if there was any means of doing so.

We were all a little quiet returning to our airfield. It was a sobering thought that on the very eve of being able at last to take the initial steps towards gaining freedom for our beloved country we must do so not as proud Polish fighters but under enforced pseudonyms.

Be that as it may, though, we are counting the very seconds until the glorious moment comes.

6th JUNE 1944

The moment has come.

I take off in a grey dawn with low cloud cover, part of a whole wing of the 2nd R.A.F. Our task is to patrol and to protect, not to attack. We carry no bombs. An extra fuel tank has been fitted instead beneath the pilot's seat and the folded dinghy. I am not very comfortable but that is the last thing on my mind.

The sea is grey with quite a heavy swell. I have always had a fear of that sea and of being forced down into its chilly depths as has happened to so many colleagues. Today it is no longer a threat. Looking down I realise that if I come down it will not be into the water but onto one of the countless ships making their way below.

Ships! Hundreds and hundreds of them, of all types and sizes. All with a separate job to do. There some floating items that I cannot identify — huge caissons on tow, moving very slowly. Giant spools also on tow like macroversions of those on my mother's sewing machine. What can they be? What possible role have they been cast for?

The sky is filled with aircraft, too. Fighters. Heavy bombers. It is imperative to keep in strict formation lest we bring each other down.

Now we have reached Ouistreham and are moving parallel to the Normandy beaches, alert all the time for enemy attack. Sword. Juno. Gold. Omaha. Utah. Each code-named beach the site for landing and attempted repulse. The sky full of fire from both sides. The coast a confused mass of landing craft, tanks and men. It is difficult to see what is happening. In the air we are above the action. Down there they are in the thick of it. It is a strange, unreal feeling.

Suddenly four Fokkers appear, diving into the unbroken cover of aircraft. My fingers twitch to shoot as I am sure do many other fingers. It is impossible. We are so closely-packed that any shots will hit a friend and not a foe. They realise the enormity of the odds against them and disappear.

We turn at the Carentan peninsula and resume our patrol back to Ouistreham where again we turn. We are on sentry duty with an appointed beat. Our fuel is getting low. We turn back across the Channel whilst a second wave of aircraft fly in to take our place. We land at Forde for re-fuelling. We are refuelled too with a huge breakfast of bacon and eggs which we have not seen for so long. Just over an hour and we are air-borne again, exactly as before. The light is better now and we can see progress on the beaches. Troops are moving inland. Landing-craft are still going in, bringing more and more men.

There are inevitable signs of casualties. Boats broken and over-turned in the water. Bodies on the beach. At Sword and even more so at Utah, there are hundreds of parachutes marking the landing of air-borne troops. There is the chilling sight too of coffins stacked on the coastline. But the tanks and D.K.W's are moving forward. Near Bayeux there is the unlikely sight of bulldozers at work making runways. Soon it seems we shall be fighting from bases in Europe. The retreat of 1940 will be forgotten and turned into advance.

We return to Forde to be put at readiness. No one can leave but we can snatch some rest. We can talk over what is happening, what we have seen.

My mind is spinning with the sheer scale of it all. We were fully prepared for our role, but it is just one piece of the gigantic jigsaw. We had no knowledge of the other pieces. Now they have come together to form a whole picture, complete and awe-inspiring. A unit from the B.B.C. has arrived to record our impressions. I try to explain, to supply the details of what I have seen.

They play back the recording. I am horrified. My speech is a jumble of Polish, English and French. I beg them to destroy it, ashamed that anyone should hear. They laugh and make no promises.

"We want your feelings to come across and they have!" they say. I do not know if what I have said will actually go out over the air. Frankly I am too mentally and physically exhausted to care.

11th JUNE 1944

We are now actually based on French soil for the first time since 1940. During those dreadful days we had promised ourselves that one day we would return and now it has actually happened. The situation has been completely reversed. Then the Allied forces were in defeat, now slowly and determinedly we are moving forward. Whatever difficult times may lie ahead — and there are sure to be many — there is hope in the hearts of everyone that the ultimate defeat of the Germans will be accomplished.

It is hard for me as for anyone else to understand the planning, the organisation, the improvisation that lies behind what is now happening. We had been able to know and to understand just one part of the huge operation — the part that we were to play — and now like some enormous jigsaw the various pieces have come together to form a complete picture with every man and woman making sure that the piece for which they have trained and are responsible fits perfectly into that picture.

For the moment our particular role seems to be a somewhat minor one. We are forming a complete umbrella over the battles raging below so that the Luftwaffe have no chance to attack. We cannot even attack ground targets for there is no distinctive line between the enemy forces and our own. It takes nerve and iron discipline to patrol the empty skies exactly as we have been ordered but we know that eventually our moment will come.

On June 8th we landed after our first patrol at the airfield near Bayeux where we had already seen the bulldozers at work. Here in shallow trenches we were given corned beef to eat and horrible chlorinated water to drink while our aircraft were dispersed to be refuelled and serviced as necessary. Jeeps took us a few miles to another new airfield — B.10 — where we saw a runway and perimeter roads being constructed in a way that was as ingenious as it was rapid. Sand was laid on the ground and covered with tar paper from enormous rolls. Tar was sprayed onto the paper and then rolled before the process was repeated over and over again to give a hard, even surface. We whispered privately that it would be useful until a Boston made an emergency landing without the benefit of an undercarriage and left damage that was as superficial as the damage to the aircraft.

We were within range of the German guns on the hills over the River Orne and we were told each to dig our own dug-out as tents alone would give little or no protection. Some of my colleagues contented themselves with shallow depressions but my scouting days were vivid in my memory. I dug a good deep hole and lined it both walls and floor with off-cuts of the tar paper begged from the construction workers plus a couple of handy railway sleepers reinforcing the entrance. I meant to be not only protected but warm and dry! Jeeps collected us for our next patrol and returned us to Bayeux where our aircraft were ready and this time at the end of the sortie we landed back at Ford.

On June 10th, however, the new B.10 airfield was ready and our days in England were temporarily over. Supplies had arrived and our tents had been erected over our dugouts covered with camouflage netting. I felt quite happy with my new home where I had my canvas bed, canvas wash-basin and canvas chair and a small oil lamp to give me light when darkness fell. I had slept in worse places!

It was not exactly peaceful. Battleships were firing salvoes from the coast and the Germans had got our range and were firing shells from their position on the opposite hills. Some of them seemed to be uncomfortably close and it wasn't long before some of my colleagues who had not appreciated the dangers of the situation and consequently had not thrown themselves with proper enthusiasm into their digging came and begged for shelter. I agreed to let them join me provided they each contributed some of the liquor ration which we had all received so quite a merry party ensued. It certainly took away the taste of that corned beef and chlorinated water and made us think and talk enthusiastically of what might lie ahead. We were sobered in more ways than one the next morning when we found that seven of our ground crew had been injured by enemy fire. It certainly set everyone busy digging really deep dugouts.

12th JUNE 1944

Our Squadron-Leader, Wacek Krol, was a wonderful leader who knew how to deal with men as well as with the war situation. He knew we were growing bored with the monotonous if necessary work of patrolling skies empty of the enemy, shaken by being fired at from the hills over the Orne with no chance to retaliate, and sickened by the same diet of corned beef and chlorinated water enlivened only by our scant spirit ration. He wanted us all to be mentally and physically alert for the tasks that he knew lay ahead and hit on an idea to address at least the third problem.

It was my turn to rest and he sent for me and asked me what I knew of aerodynamics. I could not think what the point of the question was until he said he had arranged for two barrels of beer to be supplied from the country hotel near Chichester which had been the Mess for senior officers.

"They'll fit one under each wing in place of bombs," he said, "but obviously we must find a way of adapting them for flight."

Anything for a change! I readily agreed to take an aircraft and fly to our old aerodrome near the hotel. I was sure that with some of the ground-crew we could find a means of bringing over the barrels safely and without mishap.

Sure enough the ground crew were delighted to be faced with a new challenge and between us we hit on the idea of fitting metal propeller cones over the barrels. It worked like a dream when they had been installed using bomb hoists and I flew back to B.10 feeling cheerful and refreshed. I did not like beer myself but I managed to get hold of a large piece of boiled bacon which I stowed in the cabin, smacking my lips at the thought of being able to bypass corned beef.

What an enthusiastic reception I or rather the beer received back at B.10. Gone were all the long faces, all the despondency.

A particular source of satisfaction was when some soldiers came by, saw us quaffing beer, and stopped to barter anything they had "won' in the campaign so far for a drink. It was even more satisfying that night to be told that Bayeux had been taken and that soon — very soon — we would be well and truly in action.

25th AUGUST 1944

We are back in Britain on the Gower Peninsula for ten days' rest from operations. It seems strange to have time to relax, to go where we please and do what we choose after all that has happened. I am trying to collect my thoughts and record at last some of the experiences and impressions of that next phase of my life as a Polish fighter-pilot. There has been no chance to write until now even if I could have collected my thoughts so that I could do so.

With the Allied advance on all fronts and in our area in particular with the fall of Bayeux, it had become at last possible to establish battle-lines and our patrols gave way to action. We were issued with maps on perspex marked with red and blue firing lines. The blue line marked the boundary of the territory in which our troops were still fighting, so intermingled with the enemy that any attempt to drop bombs might so easily have struck the wrong target. The red line marked the territory so far occupied entirely by the Germans and here the orders were in uncompromising contrast. Air Vice Marshall Cunningham sent us our orders:

"Kill anything that smells of Germans."

This did not mean, of course, that we were free to go crazy and do as we pleased. Strict discipline was called for and everything must be done according to Control for the red and blue lines were changing not only day by day but often hour by hour. Our squadron had its own clearly-defined area over which to operate and we were there to co-operate with and support the Army at all times.

Do you remember, Zosia, how disappointed I was that my first posting on getting my commission was to an Army Co-operation Unit? Now the lessons I had learned and the experiences I had had would prove vital. The troops I had supported then were on exercises, of course, not engaged in one of the fiercest real-life operations possible, but memories came back to me over the years and helped me.

As the oldest and most experienced members of the Squadron, Wacek appointed me to lead one Section, the others being led by an excellent pilot who had come up through the ranks and was now a Flight-Lieutenant as I was. It was our job to try and put old heads on the young shoulders of pilots who seemed to belong to a new generation and make certain that they played their parts to the full.

We had no extra fuel tanks now but bombs — a 1,000 pound bomb under the fuselage and 250 pound bombs under the wings. At the same time, of course, we had our machine-guns and cannons. Above all we had our eyes with which to see and even more vitally to interpret all that moved on the ground below.

We flew along the roads, the narrow country lanes, the farm tracks. We cast suspicious eyes on every type of trees and vegetation. We flew over isolated farms with their apple orchards, small towns and villages which might once have appeared beautiful but which now represented a threat. They looked peaceful but this was not peace — this was all-out war. From a few thousand feet, everything was spread out below us, everything was visible.

Are those tanks hiding in the hollows with only their turrets to be seen? We can take no chances. We dive-bomb and as we pull away smoke rises into the air.

Between those trees there are slight signs of movement. The trees cast deep shadows on the white ribbon of the road alongside which seems empty but deep down there is the feeling that the Germans are there. We circle and return, moving lower. Now a lorry moves slowly along the road, trying to hide in the shadows. We bank suddenly and steeply. We dive. The speedo in front of me jumps crazily — 250 — 300 — 400 miles an hour. Now I can see German troops jumping out of the transporter whilst it is still in motion and running to hide in the roadside ditches. Now my right hand presses the tit and I can hear the jolt of cannons and rattle of machine-guns from our following aircraft. On the road are fallen German soldiers and between them puffs of dust and bullet-flames like fire-flies. Bombs fall, making craters in the road and the transporter explodes in smoke and fire. I have to pull out sharply and the G-force deprives me temporarily of sight. My head does not seem to belong to my shoulders. I fly into the sun to make ack-ack fire more difficult if any Germans are alive to fire but I am not really worried. The pillars of smoke with tongues of red flame, the further explosions mean that our job has been done. We gather into formation again and resume our search for any other items useful to the Germans which we might have missed.

It is not always so easy. Often a road is defended by ack-ack. When we start to dive we can see gun barrels emitting red lights of unburnt propellant. Long lines of reddish sausages come up in our direction. Around our aircraft we begin to see grey puffs of smoke from exploding shells.

Sometimes as we dive we can hear a nervy voice yap: "They've got me!"

Some of the pilots are able to force-land, others to escape by parachute. Some return to the airfield, their aircraft peppered with holes. Some will never return.

I have become a fatalist. There is a job to be done and we are doing it, hour after hour, day after day. What happens to individuals, myself included, has completely ceased to matter. My mind has ceased to function except to carry out orders. I am completely drained of emotion.

Certainly there is no pity in my heart for the Germans and the hell we are giving them. Their carcasses rot in the fields. The ground is scabbed with black burnt-out tanks marking our passage. Terrorised, utterly demoralised troops wander aimlessly, vainly seeking shelter from the attacks of heavy bombers whilst we mop up those who are left. This is the war which they started and which alone has led to their destruction.

The lucky ones have been taken prisoner and lorries transport them to base camps along minor roads. I remember one such lorry passing right by us as we relaxed between sorties at the edge of our airfield. We sprang up and surrounded it, flaunting our Polish eagles and insignia, mocking them with a rendering of '*Lili Marlene*' and '*Horst Wessel*'. They shrank back, wide eyed and terrified, until the English corporal escorting them begged us to leave them alone. They were prisoners. Their war had finished. It was wrong to kick an enemy when he was already down. Reluctantly we withdrew, telling each other that the British code of fair

Tadeusz in a typical cheerful pose following the invasion of France.

play marked one big difference between our two nations. They had never been occupied, never suffered the inhuman brutality that we had known and to which Poland was still being subjected. They had not really learned to hate.

Nevertheless we were anxious to help a few days later when we saw a column of Allied prisoners with white handkerchiefs pinned to their backs being marched along a minor road in the German lines. What could we do to save them? I radioed to Control, asking for instructions. He suggested we might dive over them, giving the prisoners a chance to escape in the confusion, but it was just not practical. Not only were the German escort well-armed and already opening fire at our approach but that same fire would be turned without compunction on the prisoners should they try to escape. Reluctantly we turned away vowing that the day would soon come when they and all prisoners would be released.

The French suffered too as we saw when we were taken by jeep into Bayeux. They were still gripped with fear that the Germans would return and punish those who dared to show pleasure at their being relieved. There was ugliness too, born of fear — women with shaven heads being beaten and tormented because they had looked favourably on the Germans.

What we had seen so far, however, was as nothing compared to the sheer carnage of Caen, Falaise, and the Falaise Gap through which the Germans were trying to escape. This was war at its most extreme, fought with a ferocity from land and air that numbed the senses.

The blue line and the red line wavered and changed from hour to hour as we flew sortie after sortie, returning to base only to rearm and refuel. The skies were alive with Allied aircraft layers deep but when we were ordered to escort and protect the heavy bombers our role was purely nominal. The Luftwaffe had almost ceased to exist on the Western Front, its remnants fully concentrated in the East, and now our attacks were not in the air but from the air to the ground. Any danger came from ack-ack fire and not from enemy pilots.

Our task was brutally clear — to wipe out any German equipment or men that the bombers or the Army had missed. The smoke and flames were such that we seldom had a real view of what we had done. In any case I doubt if it would have registered. We were physically and mentally exhausted and our emotions were numb. Nothing really registered but the need to go on until the job was accomplished. If we had had any doubts they would have been swallowed in the odd scraps of news we had of what was happening in Warsaw, our beloved city. The Uprising had started but the promised Soviet support failed to materialise. Now our city and its people was facing unaided the full might and venom of the Germans. I had news through the Red Cross that my family and you, my Zosia, were still alive but for how long?

Perhaps it really came home to us when, the battle having moved on, we were taken to see the remnants of Caen before going to Gower. It was indescribable — the sights, the sounds, the stench. Dead men of both sides were everywhere, their bodies already blackened being carefully stripped of papers before being buried in huge pits marked with a single stake. Vehicles of all kinds were smashed, often with the occupants still inside. Poor horses used by the Germans to draw transport also lay dead and bloated. Lorries piled with loot taken by the fleeing Germans were everywhere. Every building had been reduced to rubble but from cellars underneath bemused French people emerged still fearful, still unable to believe that they were free.

There were lorry-loads of prisoners and shattered groups still awaiting transport. Amongst them we were told were conscripts from Lithuania, Latvia and other over-run countries including some Poles. These were carefully screened and might be given the chance to return to the fight on the other side.

And then at last we returned to Gower and have the chance to become whole individuals again. It seems such a contrast that we can hardly believe it.

The dear W.A.A.F. Catering Officer who had served in the First World War understands us better than anyone and is like a mother to us all. She will listen, and smile, and spoil us as much as lies in her power. Food is scarce in England now and rationing tight but somehow she manages to find meals other than the everlasting corned beef on which we have lived so long. Now, my Zosia, I can truly think of you and pray for you all. May God continue to keep you safe and grant that one day if and when this nightmare is over I can return and take you into my arms again.

10th SEPTEMBER 1944

What is happening to our beloved country and in particular to Warsaw where I was born and grew up, whose every stone I love? Where are you, my Zosia, and where are my mother, my brother, my sisters? There is so much happening in the various war zones that there are only occasional snippets of news and those are not reassuring. The Germans are ruthlessly destroying our city and its people and the promised Russian attack has mysteriously halted.

We have almost stopped discussing it with each other. Some of us had wild plans to fly across on a suicide mission and at least inflict some damage on the Germans but the authorities must have got wind of it. Our aircraft were stripped of their extra fuel tanks on the grounds that bombs must be carried but we know bitterly that the powers-that-be have decided that Warsaw is expendable.

There is nothing we can do but dedicate ourselves to the task we have been given which is to co-operate with the Canadian forces in Belgium where the battle now rages.

We flew back from Gower to Lille, to the very airfield we had strafed before the invasion. It was strange to see the scattered wreckage of aircraft which had been the result, some ours and some German. The people of Lille, unlike those of Normandy, were dour and unfriendly and we were warned that we must go nowhere unarmed. The Maquis were in the main Communist sympathisers and seemed disposed to treat the Allies as they had the Germans until the Mayor was summoned and told to make it clear that they were under British martial law and must obey or suffer the consequences.

We were quite glad to move on to Antwerp which had just been liberated. Our airfield was just inside the outer defences close to the old forts and the enemy was very close on the other side of the Schelde River. The first night we were there a V.I. flying bomb, Hitler's secret weapon, landed and blew up, luckily doing little damage although our aircraft and equipment were showered with soil and an extensive cleaning operation was needed

As before, this was not the type of fighting for which we had trained and had experience. There were no air battles, it was a matter of supporting the ground troops and keeping strictly to their Command's orders. The red and blue lines crossed and recrossed, changing from hour to hour, and our chief task was to prevent the Germans crossing to Walcheren by strafing troops along the Schelde Estuary and bombing the ferry terminal. It was demanding, exhausting work which has left little impression on me. I did my duty grimly but usually with little satisfaction.

One day Wacek Krol sent me with three other aircraft to patrol the long straight road to Utrecht still in German hands. I saw a very strange vehicle travelling at high speed and went to investigate. It was like a very high jeep with two observers facing backwards and two forwards. We tried to dive in to attack but it took swift evasive action, cork-screwing from one side of the road to the other. It was like a game of cat and mouse. Our ammunition was spent but although bits of the vehicle littered the road it was still able to continue towards Utrecht. We followed but ran into heavy ack-ack fire and were forced to return.

On another occasion I went on patrol toward the Hague and in the wooded country around I spotted a mysterious object which looked for all the world like an upended railway coach. There was smoke billowing from it. For a moment I considered attacking but last-minute caution told me to radio in with its position and to ask for instructions. I was told that it was Germany's new weapon — the V.2 being launched on London from Holland and Germany — and must get away fast. It was valuable to know its position, but attack was out of the question. I would be blown to smithereens which was the fate of an aircraft from another squadron which had opened fire.

The weather was grey and cheerless, much of the land over which we flew a sea of mud and flood where the Germans had deliberately breached dykes to halt the Allied advance. It was a time which matched the dreary greyness of our spirits.

30th DECEMBER 1944

Could you in your wildest dreams, Zosia, picture me living in a nunnery? War takes you into the strangest places, and this was one of them. We moved from the outskirts of Antwerp to Ghent airfield and our billets were in half a nunnery, the other half still occupied by nuns who were obviously not amused by the situation although as they spoke only Flemish communication was impossible. Maybe that was just as well because we were able to ignore their obvious outrage when we collected wood from the grounds to light fires for ourselves in an effort to keep out the damp, chilling cold.

The weather was not alone in being grey and dismal although the constant rain did not help. The airfield runway consisted of reinforced wire netting laid on the ground with ruts and holes filled in by ashes. Puddles often obscured it so that I at any rate took off with my heart in my mouth remembering all too well the crash on take-off from which I had so miraculously survived.

The chief gloom, however, came from the reverses being suffered by the Allies in the ill-fated assault through Holland known as Market Garden. The idea was to by-pass the Siegfried Line and head for Berlin, capturing the three bridges at Eindhoven, Nijmegen and Arnhem. It was the last which caused the problems as the town was defended by crack troops who were also established on the side of the only road where they could fire at will at the Allies.

Our task was to do what we could to help the situation by flying constant sorties looking out for enemy positions, bombing and strafing whenever possible. Unfortunately with paratroopers landing and gliders coming in with more forces the skies were restricted and we had to keep in constant touch with Command. The road was jammed solid with tanks which had broken down or come under fire and these were being towed away by other tanks to get them out of the way. Meanwhile they were a sitting target for the enemy guns. There was no chance to make a detour beside the road for there was a morass of mud and marsh. I realised how fortunate we were to be in the air and not on the ground although we were under constant fire with red "sausages" and grey puffs of smoke coming up at us constantly from all directions. Our hearts went out to the ground troops suffering such heavy losses and it was truly terrible to feel so helpless to protect them.

The failure of Market Garden meant the need to revise battle plans and now the freeing of the Schelde Estuary became the next objective. This was heavily defended by remnants of the German Fifteenth Army who occupied the islands of Walcheren and South Beveland to the north and an area around Breskens to the south. The whole area was a sea of mud, not only from the weather but from the floods caused by the Germans' breaching of dykes and river banks and any advances had to be made inch by agonising inch. Tanks and vehicles were bogged down and troops were not only at the mercy of incessant gunfire but of exhaustion and illness brought on by the appalling conditions in which they had to fight.

We were attached to the Polish forces fighting with the Canadians so were in constant communication as we flew every day from dawn until dusk giving what support we could but all the times aware that it was not enough. I am sure I was not the only pilot who craved to be fighting in my own natural element of the sky with the freedom to manoeuvre, to pit one aircraft against another as in same deadly duel. What could we do that would offer any real help? What could anyone do?

And then the day came when we got a desperate plea to help troops being mown down by a German artillery unit concealed in a large plantation near Breda. Reconnaissance showed that it would be no small task. The plantation covered a considerable area with fire-breaks between the trees giving the Germans solid footing on which they could move freely and their fire-power was clearly formidable. The trees were neither large enough nor dense enough to prevent accurate sighting on any aircraft which approached.

Wacek Krol decided that the only possibility was to commit a whole wing of three squadrons to the operation and asked me to take command with as many other experienced pilots as were available. We planned to mount our attack from three directions simultaneously so that the Germans would be confused in directing fire giving some of us at least the chance to bomb and strafe and destroy before being brought down.

We took off in a strange mood of mingled elation and grim determination. We knew that come what may we had at last a concrete challenge to meet a long-awaited chance to avenge in some way all that was being done to our troops on the ground and our people in Poland of whose fate we dare not speak but at least we would die as true fighterpilots.

The strategy worked beyond our wildest dreams. The Germans fired desperately but had no idea from which direction the threat was coming. They ran desperately from one side of the plantation to another, up and down firebreaks. Slowly and relentlessly we picked them off. There was no pity in our hearts. For so long they had fired at, killed and wounded

Virtuti Militari   Polish Forces Badge   Pilot's Eagle   R.A.F. Wings
Cross of Valour and Bar   1939-45 Star   Air Crew Europe Star   George VI War Medal

our troops — our troops — and now justice had been done. The plantation fell still and silent. We flew in low over the trees but no one stirred. We turned for home. By a miracle we had lost no one. Some of our aircraft had suffered damage to wings and fuselage but were able to make it back to Ghent.

That evening senior commanders of the Polish forces came to congratulate us on a job well done. They could now move forward until confronted with the next heavy obstacle. They were generous with their thanks but pleasant as it was to receive them they were not really necessary.

I did not realise it until the next day but Breda was to prove my swansong. Wacek sent for me and informed me that after two hundred operational sorties I had done all that was asked for and was to be sent back to England. It came as a shock and my feelings were very mixed. I had enjoyed being back with the squadron and knew that Wacek meant what he said when he thanked me for what I had done and tried to do in almost impossible conditions. I did not relish being back on non-combat duties but common sense told me that I was physically and mentally exhausted which meant that sooner or later I might fall from that razor-sharp standard of alertness essential to the job and so endanger my life or that of others.

The night before I was to leave they gave a farewell party for me in the mess and what a party it was! I was plied with drinks and plied too with all forms of packages which various colleagues asked me to take back to England for delivery. I was in a daze of alcohol and euphoria and was hardly aware of being bundled into bed by my colleagues. I was not even aware that the Germans had staged their own farewell too — for the first time in months they had pulled out a few of their aircraft to strafe our airfield, luckily with only minimal damage.

The next morning, still under the influence, my friends crammed all my possessions willy-nilly into my suitcase and kitbag and pushed me onto the jeep taking me to Antwerp from where a Dakota would take me to Northolt. It seemed I had acquired a few more presents and souvenirs in Antwerp for there were several bottles and packets to be pushed into my baggage and I had evidently put a bottle of Moment Supreme perfume into my pocket because somewhere along the line it broke and added to my distinctly odd aura. The Customs men at Northolt looked askance both at me and at my possessions and asked me what I had brought in. I told them with absolute truth to look for themselves as I couldn't possibly remember. They opened one bag, looked despairingly at the mix of dirty washing, shoes, packages and the like and finally told me to go. Goodness knows what they would have found if they had looked into the various packages my colleagues had given me but as it was all was well.

I was told that I was going — guess where? — to Blackpool and taken to the train at Euston. Blackpool! The scene of so many months of frustration and despair when I first came to England in 1940. This time, however, it was different. I was quartered in a good hotel on the South shore and in just over a week was on my way again, back to Newton.

I was given a warm welcome at Newton, particularly by Zygmunt Zakrzewski who had taken over the training work we had set in motion together and was proud to show me how splendidly everything was going. Group-Captain Swynar greeted me kindly, too, and was interested in hearing about the operations in which I had taken part. He told me, though, that my next official posting was to the Central Gunnery School which was not yet fully established but that in the meantime I could stay at Newton and more or less do as I pleased. He seemed to think I deserved some rest and relaxation.

It is strange to be free from responsibility and the strain of continual operations but this time I am finding it more pleasant than frustrating. Perhaps I was more exhausted than I realised. Time passes pleasantly enough. Sometimes I give Zygmunt help with his training and have the opportunity of flying. Sometimes I go over to see Louie or other English friends.

I spend a lot of time with Diana and her family where I am feeling more and more at home. I can cycle over the five miles to her village and always feel that I am amongst friends. I can join in some of the activities of that busy household and Diana seems to have warmed towards me. I have been able to find a car for her — a Standard Ten 1934 — which we have named Gertie for some reason. It is not as dilapidated as Little Stable which Kratko and I rescued and restored in 1941 but still needs a lot of work doing to it ready for use when petrol is not so strictly rationed.

I am able to put some of the horrors and brutality of war behind me for quite a lot of the time until something happens to bring it back into focus.

For instance, Group-Captain Swynar told me one day that I was to receive decorations in recognition of my work in the Squadron — the Virtuti Militari, four Crosses of Valour, and four Air Medals. All Polish decorations but I am Polish and all my work has been done with Polish forces. I felt quite overwhelmed when the whole station was put on parade and I was presented with them. I felt so proud but there was some sadness behind my pleasure — will I ever have the chance to return home and let you, my dearest ones, share them with me? I have had no news of you for so long now but I know that Warsaw has been practically razed to the ground and that terrible things are happening all the time. I dare not let myself think about it. I can only pray that God will help you.

W/O. GREEN. W/O. COLDRICK. W/O. JAMES. W/O. McFADDEN.
D.F.M.

W/O. COTTON. W/O. DIXON. F/O. SCHWAB. F/L. McPHERSON. F/L. HORSFALL. F/L. HATHAWAY. F/O. NICHOLSON. F/O. SHELDON. F/L. REEVE. W/O. TEMPLE. W/O. WHITE. F/O. ARMITAGE. W/O. ROSDIE. L/AC. McDOWELL.
D.F.M.

S/L. KARNOWSKI. F/L. LACEY. F/L. TRINDER. F/L. MILBURN. F/L. SPILSBURY. S/L. DRAPER. W/C.R. MILLS. F/O. PYM. F/L. MATHERS. F/L. MALDON. F/L. STIRLING. F/L. MARSH. S/L. SZUMOWSKI.
D.F.C.   D.F.C.   D.F.C.   D.F.M.

The Gunnery Wing at the Central Gunnery School, Leconfield, in 1945. Tadeusz is on the extreme right of the front row.

128

18 MAY 1945

The war in Europe is finally over.

Everyone is wild with delight and relief. It is one glorious party with church bells ringing, people dancing in the streets, celebrations of every kind. I understand but it is almost impossible for me to join in.

Our war is lost, the war which we fought so hard and so long to win. So many million lives have been laid down. In Poland itself. On foreign soil. In alien seas and skies. And for what?

France, Belgium, Holland, Norway, Czechoslovakia are free. They have their dead to mourn too but they can look forward with hope to rebuilding their lives, their shattered cities. Poland — our beloved Poland — is not free. The Germans have been defeated but our country was handed over at Yalta to the Soviet Union. Our people are slaves under a cruel domination and God alone knows what the future might hold.

It is a very long time since I felt so alone, so isolated from my colleagues, my friends, and those like Diana and her family with whom I have begun to feel at home. How can they possibly understand even if I could somehow find the words with which to explain? How can I throw even a small shadow on their happiness?

I am leading such a strange double life now. Soon after Christmas I was promoted to Squadron-Leader and my posting came through to the Central Gunnery School at Leconfield in East Yorkshire. I had spent Wigilia with 302 Squadron there and felt temporarily a sense of welcoming and belonging.

Now I really belong, I have my appointed place here, and the welcome could hardly be warmer. I have one fellow countryman but such things as nationality just do not arise. We are all fellow-pilots. We have all seen active service. There is a marvellous camaraderie between us which over-rides rank and all other considerations. I am among friends here from Ronnie Ramsay-Rae, our Group Captain, down. We have done all that was asked of us and have earned the right to relax and enjoy our lives which by some miracle have been preserved.

That is not to say that we ignore our duties in any way, just that the terrible relentless pressure has gone. We can enjoy flying again and enjoy evenings in the Mess with talk and eating and drinking. We have even learned to laugh again. There are even moments after a spell of convivial drinking when I can feel that six dark years have never been, that I am young and confident and have gone from my training into the Squadron as I longed to do instead of being posted to Army Co-operation.

On weekend leaves I generally return to Newton to see Louie and Zygmunt and my other friends, especially Diana and her family where I am always assured of a welcome. Another Squadron-Leader — 'Darkie' Draper — lives at Leicester and he is kind enough to give me a lift to Saxondale roundabout on the Fosse where Diana is waiting for me with her car. That car is very dear to us both. She has learned to drive. It has given us the freedom to get out and about within the limits of the very strict civilian petrol ration of 4 gallons a month.

It is only at Newton that the other less happy side of my life takes over. Here I am entirely with my own countrymen but there is a deep divide between us and the camaraderie which I enjoy at Leconfield is replaced by bitter argument and dissension. Even before today — VE Day — the atmosphere became difficult. The war was reaching its end and already we were faced with the need to take a decision on our future. To return to Poland or not to return?

We do not simply argue with each other. We argue with ourselves, deep down in our own hearts, and the decision becomes more and more difficult with each day that passes. I feel that I am literally being torn in two.

Before the Yalta agreement the question simply never arose. The thought of returning had been with us day after day, cheering us on in moments of acute danger and despair. We would go home to our families, our loved ones, and devote ourselves to the restoration of all that the war had destroyed. We would have the chance to put our training and experience to the good of our beloved Poland, to ensure as far as we could that we would never again be defeated.

Now that dream has been shattered. It makes it no easier that I have had no news from home for many months now. Is there anyone left for me to return to? And can I help them if I do? There are strong rumours that regular Polish Officers are regarded as enemies of the people and that we can expect condemnation rather than a welcome. We are likely to face trial and years of imprisonment with no jobs, no means of making a living, bringing shame rather than joy to those we love.

The British Government have made it plain that they will help those who wish to return to do so but that no pressure will be put on those who decide to remain. The Polish Resettlement Corps will give us the chance to train for new jobs so that we can build new lives for ourselves here in England. Alternatively we will be welcomed as pilots in Commonwealth countries such as Rhodesia and Pakistan.

Several of my colleagues at Newton are adamant that come what may it is our duty to return and it is very hard to be dubbed traitors by those to whom we have been so close. On the other hand there are those like Zygmunt who feel that the only hope is to establish a new life here and somehow — some day — bring their wives and families here to join them.

I have no wife and even if my family — my mother, sisters, brother and his children — are still alive it is impossible to think of them settling in England even if I could find a way to get them here. And Zosia? Is she still alive? Is she still the same girl I loved almost six years ago? The war years have changed me almost out of recognition as they must have done her. We would be strangers. Zygmunt is the only friend I feel I have and can talk to. He is the only one who understands and perhaps he understands a little too well.

"What about Danusia?" he asked.

Danusia is the name we have for Diana. She has been a good friend to so many of us but especially to me. I do not like her insistence on having other friends and am often moody and irritable when we are together. But what right have I to be jealous? She has known about Zosia right from the beginning and would never have allowed me to forget her. Is it hard for her too?

I know that the time has come for me to make a decision.

30th SEPTEMBER 1948

This is really the postscript to my story — of the years when I thought, fought, lived and dreamed solely in the skies. Now I have come down to earth and a whole new life lies ahead of me.

At least I am not alone. I married Diana — my Danusia — on 22nd June 1946 and daughter, Teresa, was born two months ago on 19th July. I have my own family now to work for and live for and dream for.

My family in Poland have accepted my decision not to return with love and understanding. I was able to trace them eventually through the Red Cross who put me in touch with a distant cousin who had been interned in Switzerland throughout the war. Correspondence with the West is difficult and dangerous for them and letters are very few and very guarded but at least I know they are alive.

Our future is insecure but we will face it together. Until now I have been working as Navigation Officer at Leconfield and they have been two years of happiness with welcoming colleagues. I could have applied to join the Royal Air Force but am too old to retrain as a pilot on jet aircraft and could not have been happy grounded.

Most of all, I would have had to apply for naturalisation as a British subject and this I cannot do. I love England and its people but I am a Pole and love my country passionately even in exile. One day, please God, Poland will be free and we will be able to return. I shall die with that prayer in my heart.

I have been offered, through the Polish Resettlement Corps, a two-year grant to study for my Building Diploma at Hull College of Technology. Had I not been a pilot I would have liked to be an architect but that is out of the question now and at least I can hope to work in the same field.

Today is my birthday and the end of my life in the air. As a birthday-cum-leaving gift I was given permission to take up an aircraft for a flight of my own choosing. I flew up and away into the sunlight of a perfect autumn day. The skies were a clear blue, the visibility perfect.

Free as a bird I flew across country and over the Lake District which was one area of the country new to me. It was so beautiful with the hills and the trees and the sunlight glinting on the lakes, the peaceful little towns and villages. It will be engraved on my heart for ever.

I returned to Leconfield. I landed. I said goodbye to my aircraft, to all my days in the the sky. I knew I would never fly again.

With a sense of completion rather than sadness I got into my car and drove home. Home to Diana and Teresa.

Tadeusz shed his last uniform and donned his 'demob' clothes in 1948 to begin a new life in England.